Carrying Capacity
in Recreation Settings

Bo Shelby and Thomas A. Heberlein

Oregon State University Press
Corvallis, Oregon

The paper in this book meets the guidelines for permanence and durability of the Committee on Production Guidelines for Book Longevity of the Council on Library Resources.

Library of Congress Cataloging in Publication Data
Shelby, Byron Bruce, 1948-
   Carrying capacity in recreation settings.
   Bibliography: p.
   Includes index.
   1. Recreation areas—United States—Visitors. 2. Recreation areas—United States—Management. 3. Recreational surveys—United States. I. Heberlein, Thomas A., 1945-   . II. Title. GV53.S47   1986   790'.06'9   86-8428
ISBN 0-87071-347-7

Contents

Preface

We were in Missoula, Montana, working on the second draft of the carrying capacity book. Tom turned from the window and groaned. "Ten below zero and still snowing. Maybe it'll be better by morning."

Morning came and it was warmer but not better—thirty-four degrees, and last night's foot and a half of snow had turned to eight inches of slush. One of the advantages of research on outdoor recreation is the field work—sunrise over golden marshlands with the sky full of geese, brilliant reflections of red rock walls at the bottom of the Grand Canyon, cool water plunging into a crystal pool along the Rogue River. Maybe Missoula in January was some form of divine retribution.

Our goal in writing this book was to come up with a single volume which would bring together work on carrying capacity. Ten years ago this area was characterized by individal one-shot case studies. Since that time the field has matured, with review articles, special issues of journals, a comprehensive review and bibliography listing over 2,000 references, and even an analysis of the way the literature has grown and been cited. We hope this book is a part of that maturity.

The book develops a comprehensive model for carrying capacity management and research based on in-depth case studies at six different locations around the country. It incorporates previous work on carrying capacity, but reviews the literature selectively rather than exhaustively. The model can be extended to a variety of settings beyond those discussed in the book, and even appears to work well as an approach for resource management in general.

Carrying Capacity in Recreation Settings is intended for researchers, managers, students, and others interested in resource management issues. Carrying capacity and crowding have been the focus for research in a number of disciplines, including biology, economics, psychology, sociology, and geography. This book incorporates a variety of perspectives, but the final product reflects our training as social psychologists and our belief that good research can be theoretically meaningful and solve applied problems. The first chapter presents the problem, develops the model, and then concludes with an overview of the rest of the book; we suggest everyone read that chapter and then decide what other sections to pursue.

Carrying capacity is one of the most written-about areas in the recreation management field. But, more than that, it has become a focus for the challenge of integrating human values into resource management decisions. The carrying capacity problem has forced researchers, managers, and users to work towards an understanding of the ways in which management decisions affect recreation experiences. The result has been a realization that maintaining opportunities for certain kinds of experiences requires the same care and planning as maintaining habitat for certain plant or animal species. Both are important and valuable, and both can easily be threatened or lost.

For years wilderness has been used by biologists to explore sensitive relationships in natural ecosystems, relatively undisturbed by outside influences. Similarly, social carrying capacity was studied first in wilderness because people there were more sensitive to crowding, and interference from extraneous variables was minimized. Data from some wilderness areas suggest that the tremendous growth in wilderness use may be slowing down. If this truly is a trend, it will give managers a chance to recover and solve some of their overuse problems in a lower pressure atmosphere. But carrying capacity research has already moved into other areas, where new challenges await. Decreased wilderness use clearly does not mean that recreationists have disappeared, but only that they have shifted to new areas and different activities. Sailboating in the Apostle Islands National Lakeshore, for example, has more than doubled in the past ten years, and windsurfing has simply exploded.

We have many to thank for their help with this book. Institutional and research support were provided by the Department of Resource Recreation Management, the College of Forestry, and the Water Resources Research Institute at Oregon State University, the Department of Rural Sociology, the College of Agricultural and Life Sciences, and the Water Resources Center at the University of Wisconsin-Madison, the USDA Forest Service, National Park Service, Bureau of Land Management, and Wisconsin Department of Natural Resources. Agency personnel were helpful in getting field work done, often under difficult circumstances. We are particularly indebted to the thousands of visitors to our study areas who took the time to tell us what was important to them; they truly are the "experts" when it comes to certain aspects of recreation experiences.

The manuscript benefited from the thoughtful reviews of both researchers and resource managers, including Jim Absher, Sam Alfano, Rich Bishop, Perry Brown, Roger Contor, Brian Cunninghame, Don Field, David Given, John Hendee, John Lloyd, Bob Lucas, Bob Manning, Pat Miller, George Stankey, and Joe Stockbridge. Bob Lucas and George Stankey at the USDA Intermountain Research Station provided both a place to work and great colleagueal support during those memorable weeks in Missoula. The first draft of the book was written while we were teaching a seminar on crowding and carrying capacity, and subsequent drafts were used in a number of seminars and classes. Students contributed both ideas and criticism which improved the final product. Gerry Alfano, Bob Baumgartner, Rick Colvin, Mark Danley, John Trent, and Jerry Vaske were graduate research assistants who became friends and colleagues as well as doing a great deal of work. Dena Keszler typed the final manuscript, Doug Whittaker helped with proof reading, and Neil Bregenzer prepared the index. Oregon State University Press provided a great professional staff, and we are indebted to Jeff Grass and Jack Walstad for their faith in the project and to Jo Alexander for her tremendous editorial work in turning a rough manuscript into a finished book.

This book is dedicated to our parents who have given us curiosity and a love of the outdoors, to our friends who have shared our adventures, and to our families who have shared so much more, including both the fun and frustration of writing this book.

Bo Shelby
Tom Heberlein
September 1986

Introduction

Floating through Grand Canyon on the Colorado River is a spectacular adventure. John Wesley Powell made the first expedition through the Canyon in 1869, but even as recently as 1950 less than one hundred people had run this section of the Colorado River. In the 1960s all that changed. Visitor numbers increased an average of 59 percent per year between 1960 and 1972, from 547 floaters in 1966 to 16,428 in 1972. Crowding and overuse problems were particularly evident to boatmen and outfitters who had run the river in earlier years. A petition submitted to the Park Service put it this way:

> "A Colorado River trip gives people a chance to experience the beautiful, quiet, and sublime wonders of the Grand Canyon. Let them stand alone under the great waterfall at Deer Creek and feel its power, without hundreds of people pushing, taking pictures, bathing, and filling water jugs. The Canyon should provide a contrast to the cities, with their problems of overpopulation and crowding."

Complaints such as these caused the Park Service to freeze use at 1972 levels, pending studies of carrying capacity.

Crowding and overuse problems in Grand Canyon were not unique (Hendee et al. 1978). In Yosemite National Park, backcountry camping increased from 78,000 to 221,000 overnight visits between 1967 and 1972. Between 1967 and 1974, overnight stays in Shenandoah National Park quadrupled. In the ten-year period from 1966 to 1976, backcountry use in Rocky Mountain National Park increased 730 percent, while overall use of the park increased only 73 percent.

Use figures for National Forest backcountry areas show similar trends. From 1946 to 1964, visits to wilderness areas increased about sevenfold, while population of the United States increased only 35 percent. Visits nearly doubled from 1965 to 1975, while population grew about 10 percent.

In response to this dramatic growth in backcountry use, many studies have described and evaluated recreation impacts. Much of this research fits under the generic label "carrying capacity" and is concerned with determining the number of users that can be accommodated by a given area without loss in the quality of the natural environment and/or the visitor experience.

Both the Introduction and Chapter One were authored jointly by Bo Shelby, Thomas A. Heberlein, and Jerry J. Vaske.

Scientific investigations have documented recreation impacts and factors affecting their incidence and severity. In addition, popular articles have conveyed this knowledge to the general public, and articles for recreation managers have attempted to provide a framework and/or guidelines for application of this understanding to the planning and management of recreation resources.

Concerns about crowding and resource deterioration in recreation settings can be traced to the late 1920s (Meinecke 1928). J.V.K. Wagar (1946) and the ORRRC reports (1962) provided further support for the importance of the carrying capacity concept, but major theoretical and empirical advances did not appear until 1964. At this time researchers in the USDA Forest Service (Lucas 1964; J. A. Wagar 1964) pioneered what would become a major effort to consider the impacts associated with the presence of varying numbers of recreationists.

The Forest Service's early attention to recreation impact problems stems partially from two conflicting legislative acts. The Multiple Use and Sustained Yield Act of 1960 and the Wilderness Act of 1964 mandated the agency to provide recreation opportunities but also to conserve the natural characteristics of selected environments. The early presence of the Forest Service in this field can also be attributed to the existence of previously established experiment stations throughout the nation. Because these stations had the human and financial resources, a publication outlet for technical reports, and the official mandate to conserve natural areas, the agency was well positioned to become a leader in research activities.

The frequently cited early papers that came out of the Forest Service (e.g., Lucas 1964, Wagar 1964, Hendee et al. 1968, Stankey 1971, 1973) served several functions. First, they began the process of documenting the social consequences of the presence of other visitors on a recreation experience. Second, the mere existence of these reports brought to light similar issues faced by other agencies. Cahn (1968) and others, for example, began to question whether success would spoil the National Parks. The Conservation Foundation (1972) also published several recommendations aimed at restoring the mission of the Park Service as steward of special and unique environments.

A third function served by these early articles was to legitimize the study of social issues in a natural resource setting. Prior to the late 1960s and early 1970s, university-based programs or departments concerned with environmental issues tended to focus on biological considerations. Similarly, recreation departments housed in colleges of physical education, recreation, and health were primarily concerned with activity programming, administration, and therapeutic recreation.

Since the late 1970s, however, many major universities and colleges have had at least one researcher interested in evaluating recreation impacts from a social science perspective. Associated with this growing interest in understanding the human aspects of outdoor recreation has been an increase in the number of publication outlets. In addition to the general technical reports produced by government agencies, university-based experiment stations, and private organizations, a number of technical journals now regularly include articles on the social dimensions of outdoor recreation. These include *Leisure Sciences, Journal of Leisure Research, Journal of Applied Ecology, Journal of Forestry, Journal of Soil and Water Conservation, Wildlife Society Bulletin, Environmental Economics and Management, Environmental Management,* and *Journal of Interpretation.* Similarly, specialized conferences have emerged, some with their own yearly proceedings (e.g. the Southeastern Recreation Researchers' Conference, Wilderness Psychology Group, Rural Sociological Society, etc.). This list is by no means exhaustive, but it illustrates the breadth and diversity of interest groups now actively engaged in recreation research.

Since the early Forest Service studies, numerous researchers have sought to establish carrying capacities for specific resources (see, for example, Vaske et al. 1984); proposed guidelines for sorting out the complexities of the concept (Brown 1977, Hendee et al. 1978, Schreyer 1976, Shelby and Heberlein 1984, Stankey 1979); and even questioned the validity of the carrying capacity concept for recreation (Bury 1976, Burch 1981, 1984, Washburn 1982, Becker et al. 1984). Efforts to pull together and synthesize previous work related to carrying capacity and visitor impacts have resulted in several annotated bibliographies that have examined particular related topics, such as Cole and Schreiner's (1981) bibliography on soil and vegetation impacts, Ream's (1980) bibliography dealing with the impacts of recreation on wildlife, and Stankey and Lime's (1973) annotated bibliography on several recreational carrying capacity considerations. Most recently, a bibliography by Vaske et al. (1984) identified over 2,000 published and unpublished articles on human impacts in natural environments. In spite of the volume of research that has been conducted, however, "social carrying capacity remains an elusive concept" (Graefe et al 1984b). Stankey (1980:6) states that "significant conceptual and methodological problems remain," while Burch (1981:221) goes further in suggesting that "research methodology, theory, and findings remain at a primitive level."

There is no shortage of models in the recreational carrying capacity literature. Hendee et al. (1978:169), for example, describe a "general model of carrying capacity" and its possible application to wilderness. This model deals with ecological and social impacts of increasing wilderness use, and considers management objectives and value judgments. Lime (1976:123) points out that carrying capacity has traditionally been "a management concept, a framework or way of thinking about how to plan and manage a particular recreation resource. It is not the basis for some magic formula that gives the manager the answer to the continuing question how much is too much." Because of the difficulty of making a model operational and actually helping managers make capacity decisions, some researchers (Wagar

1974, Bury 1976) have argued against the carrying capacity concept. To illustrate how a carrying capacity model works, Hendee et al. (1978) are forced to use a plausible but hypothetical example at the close of their chapter on carrying capacity.

The models proposed by Hendee et al. (1978) and others (Washburn 1982, Graefe et al. 1984a) are useful ways of thinking about the carrying capacity issue. But moving from theoretical discussions to management applications requires an operational set of procedures to arrive at a specific number. The goal of this book is to integrate theory and application by developing the procedures which appear to be most useful.

Our involvement in carrying capacity research began in 1973 when we were involved in the National Park Service project to determine carrying capacity for river running on the Colorado River in Grand Canyon National Park. Since that time, we have done carrying capacity studies involving a diversity of activities and settings. These include river running in wilderness areas, river running and tubing in developed areas, river running in a sensitive bald eagle habitat, wilderness backpacking, hiking in more developed areas, deer hunting in remote areas, deer hunting in intensively managed experimental areas, goose hunting in high density "firing lines," goose hunting in low density "managed hunts," fishing in several areas, and sailing in the marinas and islands of Lake Superior. Although we come from an academic background and share a commitment to scientific research, all these projects were done at the request of resource managers who needed to solve immediate and pressing overuse problems.

We believe the relationship between theory and application is truly symbiotic. Science is advanced when researchers take responsibility for working through application of theory, and management improves when managers discover the ways research can work for them. This book, therefore, speaks to both researchers and managers.

The model presented in this book is a practical, applied approach to social carrying capacity which builds on the existing literature as well as our own research. This approach usually provides numerical capacity estimates, and when it does not the exact reasons are clear. There is little in our model which is inconsistent with prior thinking in the field. Its principal contributions are to: (1) organize and make explicit a set of concepts, variables, and procedures for establishing carrying capacity; (2) demonstrate the utility of the sociological concept of norms as an explicit means of measuring visitor preferences; and (3) provide empirical evidence regarding the evaluative dimension of carrying capacity.

There are at least three difficulties in establishing capacities. First, people have different wants, so there are different carrying capacities for different experiences (Schreyer 1976). Second, any use produces some change, and it is difficult to tell just how much change is too much (Hendee et al. 1978). Finally, the number of users is sometimes a poor predictor of impact; even low amounts of use, for example, can severely impact plant communities (Cole 1982). The approach developed in this book deals with each of these difficulties. It provides an empirical method for identifying specific recreation experiences, and indicates the data needed to determine appropriate numbers of people for different types of experiences. By focusing on areas where people agree rather than disagree, it is often possible to establish capacities for specific experiences. The model also specifies the data needed to show whether the number of users in the system is related to impact.

As capacity studies move away from theoretical discussions toward actual applications (see, for example, McLaughlin et al. 1982), the model presented in this book is a first step. It does not cover all the issues or answer all the questions, but it does give a common framework and shows how a model can be applied.

Book Overview

This book develops a general conceptual framework for carrying capacity which can be applied to a variety of situations. The book speaks to researchers who conduct capacity studies and resource managers who make capacity decisions. Although we think this approach combines the best of science and management, certain sections may be of greater interest to one group or the other. Each chapter has a summary at the beginning for those who want only a brief overview.

Chapter 1 looks at some of the issues in nonhuman capacity research, reviews the relevant carrying capacity literature, and develops a framework for social carrying capacity in recreation settings. We have not tried to review all the prior literature, but have highlighted the material that serves as the basis for our approach.

Chapter 2 describes the areas we studied and the recreation experiences they offer. It then presents the descriptive component of these capacity studies, which defines use patterns and the relationships between management parameters and impact parameters.

Chapters 3 *and* 4 explore crowding and satisfaction, drawing on theoretical issues and quantitative evidence. From the manager's point of view, the bottom line is that we find perceived crowding and overall satisfaction have only limited usefulness for determining social carrying capacity. If you want to know why, look at these chapters; if not, go on to Chapter 5.

Chapter 5 describes the approach we have found most useful for making capacity judgments. There are some complications and qualifications, of course, but with the right information capacity can often be estimated. This chapter reports three case studies where efforts to establish capacity met with varying degrees of success.

Chapter 6 deals with implementation, application, and future research. The gathering of data alone does not guarantee that a carrying capacity will be set; the first section of the chapter identifies the issues that will help both managers and researchers decide whether a study is likely to be translated into policy. The next section shows how to apply the model to new activities and areas, and the chapter concludes with a brief discussion of issues which warrant further research.

Chapter 7 discusses the allocation issue. Solving one problem sometimes creates others, and this is true with carrying capacity. Setting a use limit establishes the size of the pie, so to speak, but then people start fighting about who gets the biggest piece. All allocation systems require tough decisions about goals and objectives. Two basic allocation mechanisms are described and their benefits in specific situations evaluated.

For those planning to become involved in a carrying capacity study, three methodological appendices are included. The first reports the measures used in our carrying capacity studies, the second deals with the broader issues which must be considered in setting up a capacity study, and the third outlines the data which are useful for making allocation decisions.

1—Recreational Carrying Capacity

Chapter Overview

The carrying capacity concept comes from a range management tradition, which suggests several parallels for recreational capacity. In both types of capacity studies, it is possible to distinguish minimum, maximum, and optimum capacities. All capacity estimates involve value judgments and the potential for value conflict. Studies of nonhuman capacity suggest that capacities can be specified, quality is an important issue which requires value judgments, and descriptive information about behavior is helpful.

Establishing a carrying capacity involves both descriptive and evaluative components. The descriptive component includes management parameters—the factors that managers can manipulate—and impacts which describe the consequences of different management regimes. Different types of capacities (ecological, social, physical, or facility) focus on different types of impact. The evaluative component involves value judgments regarding the type of experience to be offered and specific standards defining the important dimensions of that experience. Capacity determination requires integration of both components; carrying capacity can be defined as the level of use beyond which impacts exceed acceptable levels specified by evaluative standards. Establishing social carrying capacity requires knowledge of the relationship between management parameters and social impacts and reasonable agreement among user groups about management objectives and evaluative standards.

Lessons from Nonhuman Capacity Studies

The concept of recreational carrying capacity is derived from a range management tradition (Burch 1981). The idea that animal capacity can be specified in a particular setting is generally accepted by scientists, managers, and lay persons; somehow it seems easier to come up with numerical limits for animals than for people. In spite of this impression, however, Stanley (1978:171) notes that "carrying capacity is not a simple notion for the range or wildlife manager, either." Research on nonhuman populations has repeatedly noted that there is not just one definition of carrying capacity (Ream 1980).

Minimum, Maximum, and Optimum Definitions

Dasmann (1964:59) defined carrying capacity as the number of animals of any one species that can be maintained in a given habitat, yet he is careful to point out that populations can be stabilized at various levels. Dasmann presents three definitions of carrying capacity, each based on different assumptions or value judgments about the animals and the ecosystem. The first definition is based on the low point in the annual cycle for populations protected from hunting or other forms of nonnatural reduction. Using this definition, capacity refers to the number of animals which can survive a stressful part of the year such as the cold of winter or the heat and drought of summer. This capacity is essentially a minimum where the population is unlikely to be further reduced by normal biological processes.

A second definition of carrying capacity is based on the upper limit of population growth. In a given habitat, there is a maximum point beyond which the animal population can grow no more, and births are offset by deaths. The animals may not be particularly healthy or robust, but they are alive and can be counted. Caughley (1976:217) defines this type of carrying capacity as "the maximum density of animals that can be sustained indefinitely without inducing trends in vegetation." This maximum capacity is higher than the minimum capacity defined above.

Dasmann's third definition of capacity, based on maximum productivity, allows for a number of animals somewhere between the maximum and minimum. The goal here is to manage the population to produce the largest number of animals for harvest or the greatest amount of meat for consumption consistent with the conservation of land and plant resources. The habitat might be capable of keeping more animals alive, but capacity is exceeded if adding an extra animal curtails reproduction or reduces the weight of the rest of the population by more than the weight of the new individual. This limit might be labeled the maximum production or optimum capacity.

These three definitions illustrate different views of capacity as a minimum, maximum, or optimum number. In a recreation setting, the *minimum* might be the number of users or visitor days necessary to keep the facility open. Amusement parks lacking a minimum number of paying customers, for example, might close for lack of business. At public facilities, maintenance costs such as snow plowing and road grading might not be justified if use did not reach a minimum. From the visitor's point of view, there are also minimum numbers of people necessary for certain activities; for example, two people cannot play volleyball very well, and one is not enough for tennis. Attention to crowding problems often obscures this notion of the minimum number necessary to maintain certain functions, and capacity is usually expressed in terms of the upper end of the spectrum.

The *maximum* is reached when the habitat is full. When an auditorium is filled and people are standing in the aisles, for example, it is at maximum.

Similarly, a campground is at maximum when every campsite is full and some groups start overflowing into undesignated areas. If unmanaged, popular recreation areas tend toward the maximum—lots of people, with most complaining that there are too many other people. Comfort, unconstrained activities, and safety may all be compromised when the largest possible number of individuals is accommodated.

The idea of *optimal* capacity introduces several additional criteria for evaluating appropriate numbers. If people are uncomfortable, constrained, or unsafe in their recreation, then the maximum number may be too high. Capacity of an auditorium, for example, might be lowered to the number of seats available. This is an optimal or a "best" number because people can sit comfortably and use the aisles in case of emergency. An optimum level trades higher numbers for other benefits, in this case comfort and safety. In backpacking, lower numbers might be traded for greater solitude. The idea of an optimal rather than a maximum number introduces the notions of quality and values.

Value Judgments

Quality implies a subjective, evaluative judgment that says one thing is better than another. For example, one might state that more pounds of meat are better than fewer, sitting is better than standing at a concert, and seeing a few other hikers may be better than seeing more. Values become explicit when optimum capacities are considered, and value judgments lie at the heart of any carrying capacity determination.

Values complicate judgments about animal capacities, just as they do for human capacities. Caughley (1976:219) provides an interesting example. In National Parks, one management objective is to preserve a diversity of plant species. With this in mind, a park manager could specify a lower capacity for grazing animals than a range manager who might be willing to sacrifice diversity of plant species for higher animal productivity. Similarly, a range manager interested in maximum production might accept an equilibrium which included only the most nutritious plant species, while a park manager would favor an equilibrium which included a full range of native species, some of which were non-nutritive but desirable for aesthetic or other reasons.

Another case of value conflict involves the carrying capacity of range land for coyotes. For biologists who value equilibrium among species (no trends are observed and the resource is conserved), a certain number of coyotes would constitute capacity. For ranchers who value the lives of lambs over those of coyotes, the carrying capacity for coyotes is much lower, probably zero. But for a third group, defenders of wildlife, coyote capacity might be much higher.

The idea of an optimum carrying capacity revolves around the question of values, which are usually articulated in management objectives. Most of the social carrying capacity literature points out that capacities cannot be established in the absence of management objectives. The reason it is so difficult to establish a carrying capacity for range land for coyotes is that the value premise is not shared in the human community and, as a result, there is disagreement about management objectives. Situations like this are not amenable to carrying capacity estimates; a capacity can be estimated for each set of management objectives, but the real fight is over which objectives to use. Usually this is not a scientific question, although scientists can help identify and measure the values, and spell out the possible consequences of each alternative.

There is evidence to support Stankey's (1978) assertion that capacity decisions are not easy for the wildlife or range manager (see, for example, Ream's 1980 annotated bibliography). There are multiple definitions of carrying capacity, and the establishment of optimal capacity is often plagued by value conflicts. Even so, it often seems easier to come up with biological capacities for animals than social capacities for humans.

Why Nonhuman Capacities Seem Easier to Specify

There are three reasons why capacities for animals seem easier to specify. First, the value premises are more often widely shared. For example, maximum production capacity assumes greater meat production is more desirable than other possibilities, and the value inherent in maximum productivity is so widely shared in western culture that we scarcely notice it. The ideas that one species should not destroy other species and that all have the right to exist in some sort of equilibrium are also widely accepted by biologists and the general public. If a deer herd wipes out a large number of plant species, people are likely to agree that the herd has exceeded carrying capacity.

Similarly, carrying capacities for bridges, elevators, boats, and auditoriums are regularly established and posted without serious challenge. Like capacities for nonhuman species, these limits are based on widely shared and accepted values about safety. No one believes that the number of people should be allowed to increase until bridges and elevators fall, boats sink, and people are trapped in auditoriums. When the value premise is widely held, establishing a capacity is almost purely technical—but this is seldom the case in outdoor recreation.

A second reason it seems easier to establish nonhuman capacities is that the procedural details are well established. In range management, for example, technicians use a sampling procedure where a ring is tossed on the ground and the herbaceous material inside the ring is counted, measured, and classified. Conversion tables then show the numbers of animals of various species the area will sustain. No similarly straightforward techniques exist for recreation capacity, nor have the existing procedures been universally accepted.

Finally, the focus of nonhuman capacity studies has been exclusively behavioral. Researchers have measured meat production, species eradication, age distribution, mortality rates, and other variables which can be observed and counted. In contrast, much of the theorizing about social carrying capacity in recreational settings combines behavioral characteristics with psychological attributes. In his early writings, Wagar (1964) noted that the motivation of the visitor affects the impact of numbers, and Stankey (1974) and Brown (1977) discuss similar individual needs. Those seeking exercise, for example, may be unaffected by seeing others, while those seeking solitude are negatively affected, and those seeking companionship positively affected. Other studies have looked at psychological variables such as feeling crowded (Bultena et al. 1981, Ditton et al. 1982, Hammitt et al. 1982) or overall satisfaction (Heberlein and Vaske 1977, Manning and Ciali 1980, Vaske et al. 1982). While there is much to be said about these approaches, attention to individual differences and intropsychic variables quickly makes a difficult problem exceedingly complex. Animal studies focus primarily on behavior and avoid the more complex perceptions and attitudes which make establishing carrying capacities for humans in recreation settings particularly difficult.

This brief discussion of carrying capacity in nonhuman populations suggests several important lessons which shed light on carrying capacities for humans. First, even though the issue is complex and fraught with multiple definitions, it is possible to estimate capacities. Second, optimum is different from maximum, and this difference introduces a quality dimension. Third, carrying capacity reflects human values; capacity can be established only when these values are generally shared. Finally, it is necessary to describe observable behavior as a first step in making a capacity determination. These lessons are important for the capacity model developed in the remainder of this chapter.

A Basic Framework for Carrying Capacity

There is a large body of research on crowding and resource deterioration in recreation settings. In spite of this, many researchers have argued that the lack of a systematic conceptual framework to guide research and decision making has been a major shortcoming (e.g. Frissell and Stankey 1972, Graefe et al. 1984a). Our goal in this book is to develop such a framework. This approach grew out of prior theorizing about the carrying capacity concept as well as our own research in the settings to be described in Chapter 2. Many ideas expressed by others can be integrated with the framework presented here.

Establishing social carrying capacity involves a descriptive and an evaluative component (see Table 1-1, Figure 1-1). The descriptive component reveals how a recreation system works by providing answers to the following types of questions: What happens if 500 people per day enter a backpacking area? Do they spread out and never see one another, or do they crowd trails, get in each other's way at visitor attractions, and compete for campsites?

While the descriptive component describes what is happening in a system, the evaluative component defines the specific recreation opportunities the system *should* provide. For example, what is the right number of people to see in a day of backpacking in a wilderness area? Is it acceptable to camp in sight of other parties? If so, how close can they be and still be tolerated? Evaluative data address these kinds of questions. Both components are necessary, but care must be taken to distinguish them.

The Descriptive Component

Carrying capacity is usually expressed as a number, usually a number of individuals or groups in relation to time and area dimensions. Most writers refer to this variable as the *use level*. "One hundred hikers per day entering the Lost Creek drainage" would be an example of a use level.

The descriptive component, however, goes beyond simple use levels. Within recreation systems, people move around and distribute themselves

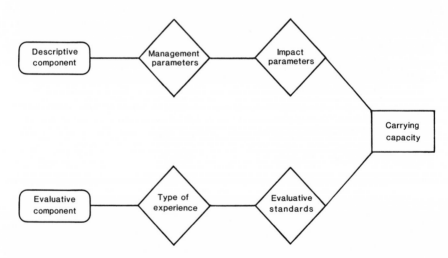

Figure 1-1. Conceptual framework for capacity determination.
Carrying capacity is the level of use beyond which impacts exceed acceptable levels specified by evaluative standards.

in space and time. They engage in different activities, such as camping or picnicking, and they engage in different use practices, such as motorized versus nonmotorized boating, or camping at established or undesignated sites. People also have different kinds of impacts on the recreation system; they affect trail width, ground cover, the amount of litter, the number of available camp spaces, and congestion at visitor attractions. The review paper by Graefe et al. (1984a) provides numerous examples of descriptive data which show how people behave in and affect a recreation system.

Descriptive data focus on objective characteristics of recreation systems, and they specify the different states produced by different management alternatives. At this level, data collected in studies of recreation capacity are analogous to those collected in animal studies; the data describe observable behavior and the measurable consequences of that behavior. The descriptive component involves management parameters, impacts, and the relationship between the two.

A *management parameter* is any factor which can be directly manipulated by managers. When managers can control the number of people in a particular area, use level is an example of a management parameter. When access is

Table 1-1. Carrying capacity framework.

Carrying Capacity: The level of use beyond which impacts exceed acceptable levels specified by evaluative standards.

Descriptive Component
Describes how a recreation system works, including physical and biological characteristics and human and nonhuman use patterns.

Management Parameters	Impacts
Elements of the recreation system which managers can manipulate. These include amount of use (use level) as well as the way an area is used (e.g. redistributing use in time or space, or changing use practices.)	Elements of the recreation system affected by the amount or type of use. The type of impact determines the type of capacity (ecological, physical, facility, or social).

Evaluative Component
Defines how an area should be managed and specifies how much impact is too much.

Management Objectives	Evaluative Standards
Define the type of experience or other outcomes that a recreation setting should provide.	Specify acceptable levels of impact in terms such as minimum, maximum, or optimum.

open by law or costs make control impossible, use level is not a management parameter. Carrying capacity information is most vital when use level can be controlled; if a number can be determined, then managers can limit use at that level.

Establishing capacities or evaluating impacts may be helpful even when use level cannot be controlled. Scientists, managers, and users may find it useful to know that an area is at or above capacity, just as similar information about wildlife on a range area is useful even if regulation is not planned. It may also be possible to affect use and impacts through management parameters other than use level (an issue discussed later in this section).

Management parameters can be measured and manipulated, but by itself a management parameter such as the number of people passing an entry point may not be particularly meaningful; we really want to know the *effects* of different numbers of people. For example, if five parties enter a river system each day, do they spread out so that no one sees anyone else, or do groups run into one another during the day and compete for campsites in the evening? What are the effects on vegetation and other parts of the natural environment?

These kinds of *impacts* describe what happens to visitors or the environment as a result of use level and other management parameters; they are outcomes associated with different amounts and kinds of use. Examples include the number of parties encountered on a trail, the number of nights spent camping alone, the time spent waiting to use facilities such as launch ramps or restrooms, and the percent of vegetation damaged or lost. In reviewing the literature on ecological impacts, Vaske et al. (1983) point out that use level is not always directly related to impacts. For example, the relationship between use intensities and vegetative cover is curvilinear, with even low use resulting in a substantial loss in the original cover (Frissell and Duncan 1965, Merriam and Smith 1974, Cole 1982). Other researchers indicate that the extent of impact is more closely related to trail design, location, and maintenance than to overuse (Helgath 1975, Bratton et al. 1977).

Management parameters other than use level can sometimes be manipulated to reduce impacts. Examples include dispersion of users to reduce trail encounters, scheduling to reduce campsite encounters, site hardening to reduce biological degradation, and education in low-impact backcountry practices. These are management parameters which affect impact parameters independent of use level. Management parameters, then, can involve changing the kind of use as well as the amount of use in an attempt to affect impact parameters. Similar arguments have been presented by other researchers (Vaske et al. 1983, Graefe et al. 1984a, Stankey and McCool 1984).

Technology is a potent tool in developing management parameters. For example, designing boats with sleeping accommodations would increase the camping capacity of beaches along the Colorado River in Grand Canyon.

In the same area, the use of portable chemical toilets rather than individual "cat hole" burial minimized the biological impact of use, as did more recently developed techniques designed to facilitate carry-out of human waste.

The first step in setting carrying capacity is to identify the important impacts, then to see how use level and other management parameters affect those impacts. Although social carrying capacity ultimately involves value judgments, documenting the impacts of different amounts and kinds of use is a basic scientific or technical task.

The Evaluative Component

The descriptive component tells how a particular recreation system works, but it doesn't give any indication of how it "should" be managed. Given a specified set of impacts, how do we decide how much is too much? The evaluative component critically considers the different objective impacts produced by management parameters in an effort to determine their relative merits. It is here that values enter the model.

A major problem in the capacity literature is that impact and evaluation are often confused. This confusion can be illustrated by the concept "resource damage." It seems reasonable that use should be limited in some way when resource damage occurs. But what is resource damage? All human use has an impact; even walking across a mowed lawn tramples the grass for a moment. But is this damage?

The term damage refers to both a change (an objective impact) and a value judgment that the impact exceeds some standard. It is best if these two are kept separate. As Stankey (1974:84) points out, "The term damage signifies a judgment that change which has occurred is undesirable. Undesirability is judged by the relationship of the change to the management objectives which govern the area."

In terms of human impact, a certain number of hikers may lead to a certain amount of soil impaction. This is a change in the environment, but whether it is damage depends on management objectives, expert judgments, and broader public values. This may seem like hair splitting, but it is not. Most carrying capacity conflicts do not revolve around resource questions, but rather around questions about values (Jacob and Schreyer 1980). In many cases we spend time and effort collecting data about the physical environment when the conflict is essentially human and is unlikely to be resolved by biological information. It is not necessary to abandon the concept of resource damage. But it is important to break the concept into two parts—the impact component (environmental change) and the evaluative component (the acceptability of the change). As Frissell and Stankey (1972) argue, deciding the limits of acceptable change is the key to determining carrying capacity. More recent discussions of the limits of acceptable change (Stankey and McCool 1984) establish consistent procedures for examining social and ecological impacts and keeping factual information about these impacts separate from value judgments about their acceptability.

Management objectives, defining the things an area should provide, are official statements of value judgments. Deciding that a given area should provide hiking opportunities rather than coal-mining opportunities, for example, involves a value judgment. The need for management objectives is a major theme in the carrying capacity literature. Lucas and Stankey (1974:14-15), for example, contend that "capacity can be judged only against the management objectives for a specific area—objectives that define the recreational opportunity (or opportunities) the area is intended to provide." Similarly, Lime (1977:124) argues that "carrying capacity can be defined only in light of objectives for the area in question."

A number of authors have suggested that management objectives need to be clear and specific (Brown 1977, Heberlein 1977, Hendee et al. 1977). Hendee et al. (1978:190) point out that "a major shortcoming in most ... management plans is the lack of objectives that allow managers to explicitly state the conditions they seek and to measure performance with regard to achieving these objectives." Heberlein (1977) further suggests that management objectives must go beyond such generalities as "protect the resource," "provide satisfying experiences," or "provide a wilderness experience." To be effective, management objectives need to define the type of experience to be provided in terms of measurable statements of appropriate ecological and social conditions (Stankey 1980).

Capacity determination requires specific social judgments about levels of impact, resulting in *evaluative standards*. Evaluative standards determine the level of impact that is tolerable (the maximum) or most desirable (the optimum). Evaluative standards are yardsticks for determining how much is too much. Suppose we find that a river use level of three parties launching per day results in one river encounter, while seven per day produces five encounters. Changes in a management parameter (use level) produce different amounts of impact (river encounters). To set a carrying capacity, we need to know which number of encounters is more desirable; we need some sort of evaluative standard.

Traditionally, some kinds of evaluative standards have been easier to understand and accept. For example, everyone agrees that water quality standards should be set to prevent sickness. Similarly, people understand being turned away from a campground when there is no more room to pitch a tent or lay out a sleeping bag, or when the parking lot is full. But evaluative standards defining important social aspects of recreation experiences have been more difficult. This is probably because it is easier for people to accept standards which appear to be based on objective data, such as those for establishing water quality, than standards which appear to be based on subjective impressions, such as those for establishing the quality of a recreation experience.

Our goal here is to develop procedures for establishing evaluative standards for social carrying capacity based on objective data. Establishing water quality, for example, involves a scientific process of gathering information about the composition of the water, and then applying a set of carefully developed standards, or value judgments, to see if the water meets those standards. The model developed in this book proposes a similar scientific process for social carrying capacity. The process involves gathering information about resource use, then developing and applying standards which define the important aspects of the recreation experience.

Standards in Recreation

The idea that recreationists use some kind of standard to evaluate a certain number of people as too many, just right, or too few, is implicit in many studies of crowding (Vaske 1978, Shelby 1980). When such standards are widely shared, they can be referred to as social norms, which define appropriate conditions or behaviors for specific activities (Cancian 1975). In recreation, the clearest norms or standards are found in games such as tennis. Here written rules specify the size of the court and the number of players. If three people are on one side of the net, social carrying capacity has been exceeded, though there is still plenty of room, and people standing on the court may not feel crowded. These standards are widely shared, even among those who do not play tennis. Tennis has rigid evaluative standards; the number on a side is not generally changed, even in informal situations.

Other games have more flexibility. Six on a side is specified in the rules for volleyball, but in many cases a range of players is tolerable, from two on a side to perhaps a dozen for a backyard game on a Sunday afternoon. Even here, however, twenty-five or fifty on a side would be considered far too many.

Other types of recreation seem to have similar rules. For example, a number of studies show that people prefer to camp away from other parties at campsites in wilderness areas (e.g. Lucas 1964, Stankey 1973, Lee 1975, Badger 1975). This is not a written rule, like those for the game of tennis, but when researchers ask different people in different wilderness areas, most say they prefer to camp alone. This standard, like the informal rule for volleyball, is somewhat flexible, but zero is the clearly preferred encounter level.

One of the difficulties in determining social carrying capacity is that in many instances there are no preestablished evaluative standards. One way to develop evaluative standards is to measure individual user preferences. When these preferences show some agreement, a shared norm or group standard emerges.

Is there agreement about the standards such as the "right" number of encounters for backpacking or river running? The normative approach outlined in this book makes this a question to be answered by empirical research. Most people agree about standards for tennis and volleyball; perhaps they also agree about standards for other recreation experiences. By gathering and examining data on individual preferences, we can find out whether people agree enough to permit us to develop standards.

The literature on carrying capacity (and on resource management in general) shows considerable concern with the diversity of interest groups and public values. Although the approach taken here represents an attempt to identify areas of agreement about evaluative standards, it does not overlook or obscure diversity. On the contrary, an empirical approach to evaluative issues puts us in a better position to identify distinct publics or user groups and to document the degree of agreement or disagreement about evaluative standards.

This approach also allows us to document subtle differences in standards within the same activity. Consider deer hunting, for example. Some hunters want no interference, so they prefer to see no one, although they may tolerate seeing four or five other hunters during a day in the field. In contrast, others believe that more hunters move deer and increase the likelihood of success. This group prefers to see fifteen other hunters and can tolerate from five to thirty-five contacts in a day (Heberlein and Laybourne 1978).

For deer hunting, a single carrying capacity based on the average will satisfy no one. Managers must provide two separate opportunities for these two groups, each with a different capacity. If there are dozens of groups all with different preferences, then clearly no standard exists, but in many cases there is considerable agreement about the preferred number of people in a recreation setting. The same basic principle applies to all recreation activities, even though the amount of shared agreement may vary. Chapter 5 presents specific methodologies for developing such standards.

Two other approaches for developing evaluative standards are found in the carrying capacity literature. Although these approaches are less useful than the normative approach outlined above, the rationales for evaluative standards based on satisfaction and perceived crowding are discussed in Chapters 3 and 4, respectively.

A Generic Definition of Carrying Capacity

With the descriptive and evaluative dimensions identified, we can propose a generic definition. *"Carrying capacity is the level of use beyond which impacts exceed levels specified by evaluative standards."* Carrying capacity identifies a number for one management parameter, use level, and assumes a fixed and known relationship between use level and impacts. The capacity will change if other management parameters alter that relationship, if management objectives are changed, or if user values change radically. Carrying capacity determinations require objective measures of the impacts of management alternatives that are distinct from the evaluations of these impacts.

This definition can be used for nonhuman as well as human populations, and it applies to capacities other than social carrying capacity. It shares some elements with earlier definitions, although there are critical differences. Lime and Stankey (1971:175), for example, define recreational carrying capacity as ". . . the character of use that can be supported over a specified time by an area developed at a certain level without causing excessive damage to either the physical environment or the experience of the visitor." "Character of use" in this definition seems to include what people do and how they do it. Our definition specifies use level as the management parameter to be established, but it clarifies the role of other management parameters and uncontrolled factors that may influence impact parameters independent of use level. "Excessive damage" in Lime and Stankey's definition is a nonspecific evaluative standard, although two general domains of evaluation (physical and experiential) are noted. The definition we propose is more precise than Wagar's (1964:3) statement that "recreational carrying capacity is the level of recreation use providing a sustained quality of recreation" or Stynes's (1977:1) notion of the "level of use activity that best achieves the given purposes of the system." Our definition is more similar to that of Pfister and Frenkel (1974:6) who define carrying capacity as the "ability of a recreational resource to support a user population at a measurable threshold based on specified goals or standards."

Four Types of Carrying Capacity

It is useful to distinguish between four types of carrying capacity in recreation settings (many writers have made similar distinctions; see Butler and Knudson 1977, for a review). These four types are differentiated by decisions about which kinds of impact are important.[1]

Ecological capacity is concerned with impacts on the ecosystem. How does use level affect plants, animals, soil, water and air quality, and so on? Research on ecological capacity in recreation settings concerns these kinds of impacts on the natural environment. For this type of capacity, we can replace the word "impacts" in the generic definition of carrying capacity with the more content-specific term "ecosystem impacts." Examples of ecosystem impacts include percent of viable ground cover, ratios of various plant species, numbers of animals observed, and coliform counts. Along the Colorado River in Grand Canyon, for example, it became apparent that burial of human waste was causing increased coliform counts in soil and water, an impact evaluated by the Park Service as unacceptable. The agency introduced a management parameter (carry-out waste) which altered the relationship between use level and that particular ecosystem impact, solving the impact problem without reducing visitor numbers.

Table 1-2. Examples of impact parameters for the four types of capacity.

Ecological Capacity (ecosystem impacts)
  Percent of specified types of ground cover
  Number of certain plants or animals observed
  Soil compaction
  Soil erosion

Physical Capacity (space impacts)
  People per square foot of flat sleeping area
  People per acre or square mile
  Camping parties per beach
  Number of people in critical areas

Facility Capacity (facility impacts)
  Number of people, groups, or vehicles per
      boat ramp
      rest room
      parking lot
      campground
  Visitor-staff ratio
  Percent occupancy for various facilities
  Time waiting to use facilities
  Number of campground refusals

Social Capacity (social impacts)
  Encounters with other parties per hour, day, etc.
  Number of encounters with groups of a particular size and type
  Percent of nights camped away from others
  Percent of attraction sites where people are out of sound and sight of others
  Number of people encountered at each attraction site

Physical capacity is concerned with the amount of actual space, so impacts can be referred to as "space impacts." On the Rogue River, for example, river runners camp on natural beaches along the river. It is possible to estimate the physical capacity for camping on a given beach by considering the impacts of different numbers of people. If ten people camp at Clear Creek, for example, each might have a 4 by 8 foot flat space to sleep, but if twenty camp there the space per person will be cut in half. If an evaluative standard suggests that each person should have a 4 by 8 foot space, then any number over ten exceeds physical capacity. Similarly, the physical capacity of a pool at a hot spring is reached when there is no room for an additional person to sit and soak. The amount of space in natural areas is fixed; the only opportunity to increase physical capacity lies in management parameters aimed at more complete or efficient utilization of space.

Facility capacity involves improvements intended to handle visitor needs, including such things as parking lots, boat ramps, developed campgrounds, and restrooms. Administrative personnel are also included in this category. Facility capacity can almost always be increased by spending money. It is possible, for example, to expand campgrounds, build additional launch facilities, or add more personnel. The impacts associated with facility capacity can be referred to as "facility impacts."

Social capacity refers to impacts which impair or alter human experiences, and we call these "social impacts." *Social carrying capacity is the level of use beyond which social impacts exceed acceptable levels specified by evaluative standards.* Impact parameters focus on the number, type, and location of encounters with other human groups, and on the way these encounters affect the recreation experience. Some social capacities seem easy to establish. If lovers are looking for an intimate afternoon together, for example, the appropriate number of encounters with others is zero and the social capacity is two. It is more difficult, however, to establish capacity for a backcountry hiking experience or a day trip floating on an easily accessible river. Social capacity has traditionally been difficult to determine, primarily due to the difficulty of establishing evaluative standards.

Examples of impacts associated with the four types of capacity are summarized in Table 1-2. Objective measures of the impacts under low, medium, and high use conditions are needed to provide a range of impact conditions for subsequent evaluation. Evaluative standards are then used to determine which level is acceptable or desirable.

All four types of capacity are important, and work needs to be done on acceptable levels of impact for each one. The remainder of this book, however, focuses on social carrying capacity. Visitors and managers are often most concerned about social capacity, and in many settings social capacity is likely to be the limiting factor. In addition, the procedures for establishing social capacity are not well established, so this is an area which clearly needs work. The framework developed here is helpful in establishing the other types of capacities, but direct work on these is beyond the scope of this book.

Conditions Necessary to Establish Social Capacity

Three conditions seem necessary to establish social carrying capacity. These are presented here as "rules" which are referenced throughout the book.

Rule 1: To establish social carrying capacity, there must be a known relationship between use level or other management parameters and social impacts.

This first rule refers to the descriptive component; we need to know how management parameters are related to impacts. It is necessary to show how visitors' experiences (as defined by impact measures) change as the number of visitors or the type of use changes. Several researchers (Frissell and

Duncan 1965, Merriam and Smith 1974, Helgath 1975, Bratton et al. 1977, Cole 1982) have pointed out that the amount of use has no clear linear relationship to ecosystem impacts. Similarly, we have worked in settings where natural variation in use level has little to do with social impacts on the visitor experience in terms of number and type of contacts with others. In this case, it is not possible to set a social carrying capacity in terms of use level because this number has no observable effect on experiences. One cannot simply assume a relationship between use level and visitor contacts; in each setting this must be established empirically. There is substantial variation within settings, and data are not yet sufficient to support generalizing from one setting to another, even when the settings seem similar (Graefe et al. 1984a).

Rule 2: *To establish social capacity there must be agreement among relevant groups about the type of recreation experience to be provided.*

Management objectives usually specify the experience to be provided, but the relevant groups must agree on this. If half the people in an area want to play tennis and the other half want to play football, it is not possible to establish capacity; we can establish capacity for one or the other, but not both at the same time. We need to resolve the use conflict problem before we can resolve the carrying capacity issue. Lime and Stankey (1971), Lime (1977), and others discuss various methods of temporal and spatial zoning which can separate conflicting groups so that capacities can be determined. Lack of agreement about management objectives and the value judgments they reflect is the primary reason for difficulty in establishing capacities.

Rule 3: *To establish social capacity there must be agreement among relevant groups about appropriate levels of social impact.*

This third rule refers to specific evaluative standards. Is there enough agreement about the definition of the experience so that standards can be set for things like appropriate numbers of encounters? Because the experience to be provided has already been established (Rule 2), the relevant groups are likely to be user groups. Total agreement is unlikely, but some degree of consensus is necessary. River runners, for example, may not all agree that a wilderness experience means exactly two encounters per day, but 50 percent may prefer two or less. Our research suggests there is more consensus here than is often believed; while it is true that individual values differ, often the differences are small. In developing evaluative standards it is important to recognize the consensuses as well as the differences.

Notes

1. Definitions of these types of capacity have varied widely, and terms have not always been used consistently. For example, Heberlein (1977) defines "physical carrying capacity" in terms of the spatial requirement needed for participation, while Gramann (1982) refers to these spatial limitations as "physical crowding." Biologists, on the other hand, have tended to equate "physical carrying capacity" with ecological rather than spatial considerations (Cole and Schreiner 1981, Tivy 1972, Verburg 1977).

2—Describing Recreation Use

Chapter Overview

Data for developing the model presented in Chapter 1 came from five different locations, where users participate in six different activities. Research began on the Colorado River, but interest in developing a more general approach led to studies of whitewater rafting on the Rogue River; canoeing, tubing, and fishing on the Brule River; deer hunting in Wisconsin; and goose hunting on a firing line and in a managed low-density hunt. While these studies do not systematically represent all recreation settings, they do provide a more varied data set than can be obtained from a single setting or activity. Chapter 6 shows how the model developed here can be extended to other places.

The chapter examines the descriptive component of social carrying capacity in each setting in order to see how use levels affected social impacts in terms of contacts with other groups. In many cases use level has a demonstrable effect on visitor experiences, so if contact with other parties is an important part of the recreation experience in these settings, managers can affect that experience by changing use levels. It is possible to specify an optimal or maximum use level if an evaluative judgment can be made about the appropriate level of contact.

The studies also show some experience parameters that are not influenced by the observed variations in use level. Camp contacts were low at all use levels on the Colorado River, reflecting an interaction between available campsites and user behavior aimed at avoiding camp contacts. This was also true on the Rogue, although fewer available campsites increased the level of campsite contact. These findings suggest that in natural settings user behavior and the availability of resources reduce the effect of use level on some kinds of contacts. Such impact parameters are poor criteria for choosing a use level because, within certain ranges at least, there is no relationship between management and impact parameters (and Rule 1 is violated).

The deer hunting study shows the complexity of some natural systems, where structural factors like the sizes of units, land ownership, and the purposive behavior of hunters combine to obscure the relationship between use level and contacts. By contrast, the managed goose *hunt at Grand River Marsh produced three contacts no matter what the level of use, illustrating the effect of other management parameters such as spacing of blinds and restriction of movement.*

Study Site Descriptions

Descriptive information is necessary for understanding an area and its potential carrying capacity problems. As indicated in Chapter 1, we need to identify management and impact parameters, develop ways to measure these variables, and describe the relationship between them. This information forms the basis for evaluative judgments and capacity determinations. Accordingly, this chapter will describe the study sites, specify the techniques used to measure use levels and encounters in each area, and present data showing the relationships between use levels and encounters.

Our work on carrying capacity began on the Colorado River in Grand Canyon. This was particularly advantageous because ongoing ecological and physical capacity studies provided an ideal context for the sociological research, the resource allowed unusually good control, managers were supportive, and the methodological and conceptual issues were relatively well defined. When the study in Grand Canyon was completed, we looked for other locations in which to generalize and extend the findings. This led to studies of rafting on the Rogue River in Oregon; canoeing, tubing, and fishing on the Bois Brule River in Wisconsin; two kinds of goose hunting at the Horicon Marsh in Wisconsin; and deer hunting throughout Wisconsin.

The Colorado River—Grand Canyon

River trips on the Colorado begin at Lee's Ferry, Arizona, far from major population centers. The first point at which passengers can debark is Phantom Ranch, 88 miles downstream, where a foot and mule trail crosses the river. Most floaters go on either to Diamond Creek (mile 225) or to Pierce's Ferry (mile 280).

Motorized trips (about 80 percent of the total) float the river on pontoon rafts 30-40 feet long with 20-40 horsepower outboard motors. They take between five and nine days to traverse the Canyon. Oar-powered craft are generally smaller (15-20 feet) and take a longer time (twelve to eighteen days) to make the trip. Most trips are run by commercial outfitters who provide equipment, guides, and expertise. A passenger pays for the trip, shows up at a prearranged place and time, and the trip is under way. Smaller groups of private river runners acquire equipment and organize and run their own trips, with party members sharing expenses.

Days on the river take on a pattern of eating, sleeping, running hair-raising rapids, floating lazily on long stretches of flat water, admiring beautiful rock walls, hiking up side canyons, and stopping at unique natural wonders. Parties stop at places like Vasey's Paradise, where green gardens are watered by springs pouring out of the Redwall Limestone cliffs, climb up to the Indian ruins 600 feet above the river at Nankoweep Creek, or stop to swim in the clear turquoise water of the Little Colorado River. Other attractions include the falls at Deer Creek, the ferns, flowers, and grottoes at Elves' Chasm, and the terraced blue pools at Havasu. Many visitors have heard about these spots because they are described in most guidebooks.

People develop a sense of intimacy with the desert and the river. The days are hot and the water cold. Sand is everywhere and inevitably sifts into hair, clothes, gear, and food. The river provides an ideal way to visit this wild area because boats support the loads, hikes are optional, beaches provide soft sandy places to sleep, it seldom rains at night, and there are few insects. The river is always available when the sun gets too hot, and it keeps drinks cold as well.

Data collection on the Colorado River. Data were collected during the summer of 1975. The sample of 46 trips (39 commercial and 7 private) represents river trips from April to October 1975 (see Shelby 1976 for details). Observers recorded river, attraction site, and campsite contacts for over 475 days on this river. At the completion of the trip, each passenger was asked to fill out a questionnaire. Questionnaires were completed by 1,009 passengers, 96 percent of those on the sampled trips. Additional data were collected from people who attended public meetings in 1978 regarding the draft management plan.

The Rogue River

The Rogue River rises in the Cascade Mountains in southwestern Oregon and flows about 180 miles to the Pacific Ocean at Gold Beach. Roads and towns are built along much of this distance, but the unique character of the river was recognized in 1968 when 84 miles were declared part of the Wild and Scenic Rivers System. About 40 miles of this section, flowing through the Siskiyou Mountains, was classified "wild," with the river essentially preserved in its natural condition. The banks vary from steep forested slopes to vertical rock walls, and challenging rapids are connected by slower stretches and deep pools. Private lodges and cabins are located in several places along the river, many reached only by boat or trail.

The scenery, rapids, easy access, and possibility for two- to five-day float trips, combined with the boom in whitewater rafting and kayaking in the early 1970s, have all served to increase float use on the Rogue (from approximately 2,800 people in 1971 to 10,836 in 1976). As use increased, managers and users became concerned about crowding. Unfortunately, regulation was complicated by overlapping agency jurisdictions and political pressure from local users.

It is about 40 miles by river from the put-in at Grave Creek to the take-out at Foster Bar. The trip takes two long days or three more leisurely ones, although some people take four or five days and spend more time relaxing or exploring on shore. Rafts are smaller than in Grand Canyon, usually 15-18 feet long. Hardshell and inflatable kayaks (the latter dubbed "orange torpedoes") are common, as are drift boats built along the lines of ocean-going dories.

The ambience is something like a Grand Canyon float trip except for more frequent contacts with other groups, less spectacular scenery, and smaller rapids. The shorter length of the trip also reduces the feeling of going on an expedition. Attraction sites are rest stops, swimming holes, and points of interest rather than the wonders of nature found in the Grand Canyon.

Below Blossom Bar, the last major rapid on the Rogue, jet boats enter the picture. Jet boats are 20-35 foot motorized craft propelled with a jet drive which forces water out the stern. They start on the coast at Gold Beach and bring tourists 52 miles upstream, the last 12 miles in the wild section of the river. They roar by at water-skiing speed, shattering any illusion of a wilderness expedition and sometimes provoking hostile responses from floaters.

Data collection on the Rogue River. Data were collected during the two-month period from June 21 to August 20, 1977. A stratified random sample of 34 commercial trips was selected to represent varying use levels during this time. Observers accompanied trips and collected contact data for more than 130 days on the river. At the end of the trip, each passenger was asked to complete a short questionnaire, and 343 (97 percent) did so. A more extensive follow-up questionnaire was later mailed to study participants (for more detailed information, see Shelby and Colvin 1979a).

The Bois Brule River

The Colorado in Grand Canyon is a unique river in a class by itself, while the Rogue is more typical of western whitewater rivers where rafting is common. Both offer opportunities for multiday trips. The Bois Brule River in northwestern Wisconsin offered a contrast to the Colorado and Rogue because it was primarily a day-use river, with canoeing, inner tubing, and trout fishing. The Brule provided an opportunity to test the generality of the carrying capacity model.

The Brule is a classic northwoods river. Its dark, clear water flows through shallow pools, bounces over easy rapids, and occasionally drops over rock ledges. On either side are high banks with white pines, broken by occasional alder swamps. In some stretches there is no development, but in others there are old log cabins and large rustic estates. Five highway bridges and several private footbridges cross the river, and two campgrounds adjoin it. This is not a remote wilderness.

The Brule has long been a stronghold of dry fly anglers (16,000-26,000 per year). Canoeing activity grew in the late 1960s, and the Wisconsin Department of Natural Resources (DNR) estimated that 13,000-16,000 people canoed the river each year between 1971 and 1976. In the early 1970s, people began to float some stretches in inner tubes, and by 1973, the DNR estimated 6,500 tubers per summer. In short, fishing pressure was sustained, canoeing increased significantly, and tubing gained popularity as a new activity.

For most canoers, the trip begins between 10:00 a.m. and noon at the Stones Bridge Landing. On busy days the small parking lot is jammed as groups line up to launch, and two rental outfits bring in vans and trailers loaded with canoes and paddlers. Trips leave about every ten minutes, most of them day trips lasting three to six hours. A typical party consists of eight people in two or three canoes. Many are novices using rented boats, and canoes often crash from one bank to the other as first-time paddlers struggle for control.

The rustic lodges along the river give a feeling of northwoods elegance from a bygone era. Floating past these is something like sightseeing in a wealthy neighborhood. The experience involves a low-key float through an elegant rustic area rather than the more demanding wilderness adventure found in Grand Canyon.

After about three hours canoeists reach the highway bridge at Winneboujou, and some take out there. Almost all the tubers put in there. Tubers bounce down the rapids in groups of two to twenty, often towing a cooler filled with beer or pop. The section from Winneboujou Bridge to the DNR campground has several more rustic lodges and one footbridge, while the section from there to the Highway 2 bridge has higher banks with alder thickets and few buildings. Almost all users get out at Highway 2.

Anglers who are not from cabins or estates along the river either float in canoes or park where the road comes close to the river and wade the shallow river in hip boots. Wading anglers represent a challenge for novices having trouble controlling their canoe. With some skill it is possible to avoid them and slip past quietly on the opposite bank, but many canoers float broadside through the fishing hole as the angler dodges the boat.

Data collection on the Brule River. It was not possible to put observers on Brule River trips, so interviewers were located at the four take-out points between Stones Bridge and Highway 2 from 11:30 a.m. until 7:30 p.m. Data were collected on 24 days beginning August 9 and ending September 1, 1975. Less than 3 percent of those contacted refused to fill out the questionnaire, and 2,965 field interviews were completed. A sample was drawn from this group, weighted to overrepresent the low-use days, and these individuals were mailed a follow-up questionnaire (for further details see Heberlein and Vaske 1977).

Deer Hunting in Wisconsin

The Brule River was chosen because it was significantly different from the Colorado and Rogue rivers, and for the same reason we sought another activity in a different setting to see how well the carrying capacity model would generalize to other types of recreation. In 1976-77, wildlife managers in the Wisconsin DNR were developing plans to reduce what they felt were crowding problems during Wisconsin's deer-hunting season. In 1975, nearly 600,000 hunters took to the field armed with high-powered rifles and shotguns for a nine-day deer-hunting season in late November. On opening day there were a few areas with over fifty hunters per square mile and many more with thirty hunters per square mile.

Deer hunting in Wisconsin is extremely important to hunters. Almost a quarter of those surveyed said they would miss deer hunting more than all their other interests if they had to give it up (only 3 percent of the Brule River canoers were so committed). About 70 percent of the hunters said that most or all of their friends hunt deer. Boys begin to hunt with their families at an early age and often return during the season after they have grown and left home, and the northern part of the state has a long tradition of deer camps where groups of four to twenty men and boys gather. For most hunters, deer hunting is essentially a day trip into the woods, usually on opening day.

The deer-hunting day begins at 4:30 to 6:00 a.m. There is no central place of departure as there is on rivers. On some public lands hunters congregate in parking lots and disperse from there, but many park their cars along roadsides or in farmers' fields or yards.

As the day wears on, hunters begin to move. People in the same party may go to someone else's stand to visit briefly, and at noon some hunters leave for lunch and return later. Some unsuccessful parties will drive to a new location at midday. All this movement results in contacts with other parties, and visibility is increased by hunters' brightly colored safety clothing. Opening day ends at 4:30 p.m. and hunters head for their cars, cabins, tents, or homes.

Data collection for deer hunting. A sample of 300 hunters was selected at random from the 1976 DNR license records. The day after the 1977 deer hunting season ended, this group received a questionnaire in the mail. There was an 80 percent response rate and 240 completed questionnaires were returned (for more details, see Heberlein and Laybourne 1978). The questionnaire measured carrying capacity variables as well as others of interest to managers.

Goose Hunting: The Firing Line

Waterfowl hunting in Wisconsin takes place around marshes or other wetlands, rather than all over the state like deer hunting. During the past two decades, wildlife managers have been rebuilding the flock of Canadian geese in the Mississippi flyway by creating a series of refuges where hunting is not allowed. Of the many places geese can choose to fly out of the refuges to feed, they seem to consistently pick certain locations. Hunters congregate at these spots and, as the geese fly over, the hunters let loose with shotgun barrages. These situations have been appropriately dubbed "firing lines." As part of a study of a low-density "managed" hunt (to be described later), we worked with the Wisconsin DNR to gather use levels and contact data on a firing line at the Grand River Marsh, about 40 miles north of Madison, Wisconsin.

Goose hunting takes place early in the morning, and cold, grey, windy mornings are best because the geese fly lower. Cars begin moving into the parking lot on a hill near the marsh about 5:00-5:30 a.m., an hour before sunrise, when shooting hours begin.

The first hunters to arrive place themselves along the refuge boundary about 40-50 yards apart, which means there is room for only a few of them along the firing line. However, hunters arriving later fill in the gaps, and soon they are spaced only 30 feet apart. Those arriving later still stand behind the first row, usually placing themselves in the gaps between the front-line hunters. There is some jockeying for position and even verbal negotiation about where to stand. There may be as many as 130 hunters in a 4-acre area, although marsh grass and camouflage clothing obscure many of them.

In spite of constant hunting pressure and apparently in defiance of behavioral psychology, the geese fly daily across nearly the same spots. Sometimes the flock goes wide, and sometimes they are obviously too high, but most often they fly at 60-70 yards, just the outer range of effectiveness for a shotgun. The hunters jump up and fire, and from a distance it sounds like popcorn during those furious seconds when every kernel is exploding. Most often no birds drop because the altitude takes the power out of the shot, but occasionally a bird will drop from 60-70 yards, reinforcing the hunters' tendency to shoot at birds that are really out of range (called "skybusting").

Occasionally flocks come over at 50 yards, which is within range, and birds tumble from the sky. When several people shoot at the same bird, it is difficult to tell who it belongs to; it is possible that all have fired a lethal shot, and stories of conflict over downed geese abound. A second kind of conflict occurs when front-line hunters fire at geese initially within range. The flock gains altitude rapidly, so hunters in the second and third ranks can't get a good shot. These hunters shout at the front ranks to hold their fire, and in the worst situations there may be shooting matches between waves of geese.

Goose Hunting: The Managed Hunt

The managed hunt took place at the same refuge as the firing line hunt, so there were similarities in terms of the resource area, the season, and the time of hunting. But there were important differences involving regulation and control. The managed hunt was announced in newspapers and on radio because new regulations had not yet been issued. Hunters had to decide between August 1 and September 10 to participate in the October-November hunt, a hunting partner had to be named, and it was not possible to specify the day one wished to hunt because this was assigned by the DNR. In spite of the low public visibility, the need for advanced planning, and some uncertainty, the agency received enough applications to assign most available blinds for every day of the hunt. Permits were mailed out with an assigned date and maps of the area.

At 5:30 each morning there were ten to twenty cars in the brightly lit parking lot, and hunters lined up at the check-in station to get their blind assignment. Most hunters then drove to nearby parking lots and walked to their blinds in the predawn.

The DNR had mowed wide trails through the brush and marsh grass to each blind. Blinds had a high wall of ten or twelve bales of straw facing the marsh, with low sides made of two or three bales. Hunters had a general sense of the location of several other blinds, although most were screened from each other and they were usually more than 100 yards apart. Because the DNR assigned only twenty of the thirty blinds each day and there were some no-shows, nearby blinds were often empty.

Because there was no competition when geese flew over, hunters held their fire until birds were very close, and shots were more likely to hit a bird. When birds were downed, however, the tall grass in some areas made it hard to find them and the retrieval rate was lower on the managed hunt than it was on the firing line. In general, hunters in the managed area were less likely to shoot, more likely to hit a bird when they did shoot, and less likely to find a bird they had shot.

Data collection for goose hunting. Because the firing line and managed hunt were adjacent, data collection took place simultaneously at the two locations. Data were collected for 41 days between October 2 and November 6, 1978, except for a five-day period from October 9-13 when the area was closed. For the firing line, random starting times were selected and an observer would go to the parking lot, count the cars, and then interview the first twenty hunters leaving the site. A total of 445 hunters were interviewed, about a 75 percent response rate. At the managed hunt hunters completed a questionnaire as they checked out, and 913 filled out this questionnaire (a 100 percent response).

Use Levels and Encounters

Social carrying capacity specifies a number for a single management parameter, use level, and focuses on impacts described in terms of encounters with other groups. The rest of this chapter describes use levels, encounters, and the relationship between use levels and encounters in each of the study areas.

Use Levels

Measuring use levels is a way of answering the question "How many people are using the resource?" Most managers are familiar with use measurement, usually in a form such as "6,200,000 people visited Grand Canyon National Park in 1976" or "The North Fork Campground got 2,700 visitor-days of use last summer." These kinds of figures may help establish use trends over time, but are not much help in determining carrying capacities because they are aggregated over such large areas and/or such long periods of time. Because such figures give little insight into the amount of use in a particular area at a particular time, more specific information is usually needed.

The Colorado River. Use levels which are helpful in determining carrying capacities can be measured in a number of ways. In the simplest case, an area has one entry point and a managing agency keeps records of use. This is the situation for river runners in the Grand Canyon, where Lee's Ferry provides the only road access between Glen Canyon Dam 15 miles upstream and Diamond Creek 225 miles downstream. A Park Service ranger keeps records of all departing trips.

Because there was substantial variation in the speeds of motor and oar trips, motor trips overtook oar trips which had left several days earlier. To better represent this, use levels were calculated for a seven-day period, including the trip departure date plus the three days before and after. Measures for both people and trips per week were included, but the units

Table 2-1.   Use levels in study sites.

Location	Units	Range of Use Levels				Average
		Low[a]	Medium[b]	High[c]		
Grand Canyon	People/week	80	400	700	950	660
	Trips/week	6	20	30	36	26
Rogue River	Trips/day	1	4	9	23	8
	People/day	28	60	90	169	82
Brule River	People/day	15	74	150	308	173
Deer hunters	People/sq. mile	1	7	15	80	
Goose— firing line	Cars/day	13	29	50	85	45
Goose— managed hunts	People/day	13	21	25	31	23

[a]The divisions high, medium or low are somewhat arbitrary. These divisions roughly divide the user population into thirds, and they are used in subsequent analyses. "Low" represents a range from the figure in column 1 to the figure in column 2.
[b]"Medium" represents a range from the figure in column 2 to the figure in column 3.
[c]"High" represents a range from the figure in column 3 to the figure in column 4.

turned out to make little difference because the two measures correlated almost perfectly (r = .94).

For purposes of analysis in this and other chapters, use was divided into three categories for each study area (see Table 2-1). Low use at Grand Canyon is 80-400 people per week, medium use is 401-700, and high use is 701-950. The average is 660 people per week. Assuming these weekly average use levels were maintained throughout a twenty-week season, the seasonal use range represented by the study is from 1,600 to 19,000. This spans the range of actual use levels from 1966 (1,067 people) to 1972 (16,428 people).

The Rogue River. Measuring use levels on the Rogue involved a similar strategy. Bureau of Land Management personnel were on duty at the Grave Creek launch site, and they recorded use each day. Rogue River trips are shorter than those in Grand Canyon, and all are oar powered, so there is less variation in travel speed and parties are less likely to overtake one another. As a result, the number of people or trips leaving in a single day is a more appropriate use level for establishing capacity than the weekly use level in Grand Canyon. There was less congruence between people per day and trips per day than in Grand Canyon (r = .75, p < .01), probably because the range in trip sizes was greater.

The trips per day measure was more highly correlated with encounter levels, so it was used for most carrying capacity calculations. It often had to be translated to people per day because river managers had been regulating use by number of people. The Rogue case demonstrates the value of recording several use level measures and then experimenting with different ones when analyzing the data or converting from one to another to clarify measures.

The float season on the Rogue runs from Memorial Day to Labor Day, although there is considerable fishing activity in the fall. During the study period an average of eight trips left each day, although use peaked on Fridays and Saturdays when private groups arrived for weekend trips. In terms of individuals, the average was 82 people per day, with a minimum of 28 and a maximum of 169 (see Table 2-1).

The Bois Brule River. On the Brule there were numerous access points and no agency was actively managing the river, so researchers had to collect the use level data. Interviewers were on duty all day at take-out points, so counting the number of people coming off the river was easy and accurate. We experimented with a time-lapse camera and an electric eye counter, but these proved less satisfactory. The electric eye correlated with interview (r = .85, p < .001), but coding from the films was time consuming. Automated counters may require more work in the long run and also may be less accurate.

Use level varied by time of day, with fishers more likely to be on the river in the morning and canoers and tubers in the afternoon. Use also varied by day of the week, with canoers and particularly tubers more likely to visit on weekends. The number of fishers interviewed did not vary by day of the week. Use level was measured as the total number of visitors per day regardless of activity type.

Deer hunting. The state of Wisconsin is divided into 93 deer management units, and surveys of game habitat and records of deer harvests are kept for each one. Deer management units are large. The average is 596 square miles, and they range from 8 to 1,825 square miles. Because the DNR already kept records of the number of hunters per unit and the sizes of the units were known, use levels were measured as the number of hunters per square mile. In the average unit there were eleven hunters per square mile, with a range from a low of two to a high of fifty-five per square mile.

These figures reflect some of the problems of many density measures. Although they are the best available, they represent areas which are large, uncontrolled, and varied. As a result of factors such as access, private property restrictions, or purposive hunter behavior, people may have been concentrated in some parts of a unit while other parts were virtually empty. The measures are not specific enough to reflect uneven distribution.

Goose hunting. The density measures for the goose hunter studies were fairly straightforward. For the firing line, we counted the number of cars in the parking lot each morning, using random starting times between 7:30 and 9:30 a.m. On an average day there were 45 cars in the parking lot; with an average of 1.5 persons per car, use level would range from about twenty to 130 hunters per day.

For the managed hunt, all hunters had to check in at one location, so it was simple to use DNR records to calculate the number of hunters in the area on any given day. The number of hunters ranged from thirteen to thirty-one per day (see Table 2-1).

Encounters

Use figures by themselves do not mean much. Knowing that 950 people left Lee's Ferry during a given week does not tell us how many people river runners will see, where encounters will occur, or to what extent congestion will force changes in planned stops or camps. Even a figure like the number of hunters per square mile on opening day, which sounds fairly specific, does not provide a clear indication of what those hunters will experience. Measures of experience parameters are intended to paint a more complete picture, showing the impacts of different use levels.

The experience parameters used here involve encounters. These studies measured encounters in several locations: on the river, at major rapids, at visitor attraction sites, at camps, and in the woods or marshes. It is important to note that the idea of measuring social impacts in terms of experience parameters can be extended to variables other than encounters (e.g., time spent waiting to run a rapid or the number of opportunities to shoot at game). The best strategy is to use a variety of measures, focusing on whatever forms of impact have the greatest relevance for the experience in question.

In the studies described here, encounters have been measured one of two ways. The first is by a participant observer who was part of the research staff. This essentially means following people during the time they are in the study area and counting the number of contacts they have with other individuals or groups. The advantages of this method are that observers can be trained to use standardized definitions of encounters, all encounters are recorded, and each one can be described in terms of location, length, other party type, the amount and kind of greetings which took place, etc. The result is a complete and generally reliable record of interactions. We have called this measure *actual encounters*.

The primary disadvantage of measuring actual encounters is feasibility. Following people is expensive, especially when they remain in the study area for a long period of time, and in some settings it is simply not possible. It was possible to place observers on river trips on the Colorado and Rogue Rivers because departure schedules were known and the person in charge of the trip could be contacted in advance. On the Brule, however, this was impossible because there were no departure schedules and an observer could not unobtrusively accompany small tubing and canoeing parties. Trying to go along with hunters in the woods would have been a similar intrusion. Another disadvantage of measuring actual encounters is that people are probably unaware of some of the contacts which a trained observer sees and records, so although actual encounter level is a fine objective measure, it does not tell the extent to which interactions are consciously perceived by others, and as a result affect experiences.

The second way of measuring encounters is to ask users to report them, hence the term *reported encounters*. The simplest approach is to use a brief questionnaire as people leave the study area, although more extensive trip diaries have also been used. In a study of trips on the Illinois River in Oregon, Shelby and Colvin (1981a) had no trouble getting users to fill out diary forms in return for a five dollar payment. Analysis suggests that diary encounter measures are more like reported encounters than actual encounters (see Shelby and Colvin 1981a).

The obvious disadvantage of encounter reports is that users will not report as accurately or extensively as trained observers. Users report only what they perceive, remember, and then tell about, so some error will be introduced into the measurement process. In addition, it is not possible to obtain extensive information about the other party, the location and nature of the interaction, and so on. The main advantage of measuring reported contacts is that it is less expensive and can be done in almost any setting. It also tells the number of encounters from the user's point of view, which may be different from an observer's.

Whenever possible, researchers should measure both actual and reported encounters and explore the relationship between the two, as we did in the Rogue River study. In the Grand Canyon, actual river and attraction site encounters were recorded during the day and camp encounters were recorded each night. On the Rogue, we used all the actual encounter measures developed in Grand Canyon, but also measured reported encounters by asking users at the end of the trip to tell us how many other river parties they had seen each day.

The other studies used reported encounters only. Brule River users were asked at the end of their trip to report the number of canoers, tubers, and fishermen they had seen during the day. Wisconsin deer hunters were contacted by mail after the season, so they were asked to report the number of hunters they had seen on opening day. Goose hunters, who were contacted as they left the marsh area, reported the number of hunters seen during the day. For each area, the numbers of contacts in the low, medium, and high contact categories are shown in Table 2-2.

The Colorado River. Less than 9 percent of the Colorado River runners had complete solitude (see Table 2-3). Over 80 percent saw one to five parties per day, and 10 percent saw six to ten. Overall, the average number of river contacts per day was slightly more than three (see Table 2-2).

Attraction sites foster contacts because parties often stop for quite a while and other parties, unwilling to miss the stop, move in. On the average, other parties were seen at 46 percent of the attraction sites. At some of the most popular sites, encounters occurred 85 percent of the time.

Table 2-2. Encounter levels in study sites.

Location	Type of Contact	Range of Encounters			Average
		Low[a]	Medium[b]	High[c]	
Grand Canyon	Parties/day	0	2.9	4.9	10	3.4
Rogue River	Parties/day (actual)	4	8.9	11.9	24	10.5
	Parties/day (reported)	1	3.9	6.9	20	5.0
Brule River	People/day	0	10.0	24.0	90	20.3
Deer hunters	Hunters/day	0	6.0	12.0	30	8.4
Goose—firing line	Cars/day	0	15.0	30.0	50	24.3
Goose—managed hunts	Hunters/day	0	2.0	4.0	8	3.0

[a]The divisions high, medium or low are somewhat arbitrary. These divisions roughly divide the user population into thirds, and they are used in subsequent analyses. "Low" represents a range from the figure in column 1 to the figure in column 2.
[b]"Medium" represents a range from the figure in column 2 to the figure in column 3.
[c]"High" represents a range from the figure in column 3 to the figure in column 4.

Table 2-3. Percentages reporting different numbers of interparty contacts in five study areas.

Location/Activity	Number of Contacts Per Day				
	0	1-5	6-10	11-20	21+
Colorado River[a]	8.8	80.9	10.3	0.0	0.0
Rogue River					
Actual	0.0	6.7	47.7	44.3	1.2
Reported	0.0	79.6	13.6	6.5	0.3
Brule River[b]					
Canoers	0.4	13.9	17.1	26.6	42.1
Tubers	3.9	14.7	18.0	25.6	37.8
Fishers	5.1	24.8	16.2	20.5	33.3
Wisconsin hunters					
Deer	9.5	38.9	18.7	24.0	9.5
Goose—firing line	0.2	5.5	12.9	29.1	52.5
Goose—managed	25.2	58.9	15.9	0.0	0.0

[a]Contacts on the Colorado and Rogue rivers were measured by observers. All other studies used reported contacts.
[b]These are *total* contacts with all other recreationists for each subsample: canoers, tubers and fishers.

Observers spent 444 nights camped along the river during the 1975 season. Only forty of these (9 percent) were spent within sight or sound of another party. Complete solitude is uncommon on the river or at attraction sites, but it is more likely to occur at campsites. Camp contacts tend to occur at certain bottleneck areas in the canyon, where there are few campsites and everyone tries to camp near popular attractions (Shelby and Nielsen 1976b).

The Rogue River. Contact with an entire party was the unit of analysis on the Rogue, as it was on the Colorado. This is the only study where both actual and reported encounters were recorded, and some tables in this and other chapters will present Rogue River data for both actual encounters recorded each day by observers and reported encounters recalled by passengers at the end of the trip.

Contact levels on the Rogue were much higher than on the Colorado. No visitors made the trip with zero encounters (see Table 2-3). An average of five parties a day was reported (see Table 2-2). However, actual encounters were higher than this.

Possible reasons for the discrepancies between actual and reported encounters are discussed in Shelby and Colvin (1981b). At low levels of contact (between four and six encounters a day) visitors are accurate reporters. At higher levels, however, it appears that they simply lose track or do not attend to the encounters, and as a result they tend to underreport by about half. The psychological process by which one notices and evaluates a contact in a recreation setting is a topic for further research.

Campsite encounters on the Rogue were also more prevalent than on the Colorado. Observers spent 98 nights on the river, and about 35 percent of the time their party camped within sight or sound of another party. For a third of these, two or more parties actually camped on the same beach. Contacts at attraction sites were, however, a bit lower on the Rogue than on the Colorado. The likelihood of encounters at the four most popular stops ranged from 31 to 62 percent.

The Bois Brule River. On the Brule it was not possible to put observers on trips, so we had to rely on user reports of encounters. Canoers did not know that they would be asked to recall the number of encounters, so we used broad categories for their responses. The Brule also called for different units for measuring contacts. People do not travel in distinct, observable parties as they do on the Colorado or Rogue, so each encounter with an individual canoe, tuber, or fisher was counted as one contact.

Almost everyone had contacts with canoes and almost all canoers had encounters with anglers. Most visitors saw no tubers, but when hot weather attracted them to the Brule, tubers came in droves.

Deer hunting. An encounter was defined as seeing one individual hunter who was not a part of one's own group. About 10 percent of the deer hunters saw no one in the woods on opening day, while 10 percent reported seeing more than twenty other hunters. These contact levels are comparable to encounter rates on the Brule River. They are difficult to compare to Rogue and Grand Canyon contacts because party contacts rather than individual contacts were measured in those studies.

Goose hunting—firing line. Not surprisingly, the firing line has the highest level of encounters of any area we studied (see Table 2-3). Less than 20 percent saw one to nine other hunters, and over 50 percent reported seeing more than twenty.

Hunters reported seeing fewer hunters than we estimated to be in the area, based on car counts. This could be a result of the tendency to underreport noted earlier, or perhaps the firing line area is large enough that few hunters actually see all the others in the vicinity. Foliage also has some screening effect, and hunters dress in brown and stay low in the grass to hide from the geese.

Goose hunting—managed hunt. Due to blind spacing and the managed nature of the hunt, contact at the managed hunt was the lowest of any of the areas studied (see Table 2-3); 25 percent saw no other hunters while hunting. No one reported more than ten other hunters, compared to over 80 percent on the firing line.

Use Levels and Contacts

Having described the use and contact levels at the study sites, we are now ready to examine the relationship between these two variables. How does the number of people using an area affect the impact measures which describe important aspects of the experiences of users? Setting social carrying capacity requires a known relationship between management parameters (such as use level) and social impacts (such as encounters), as established by Rule 1.

There are two ways to report this kind of relationship. Specifying the average number of contacts at low, medium, and high use seems most useful for managers. In addition, correlation coefficients show how well use level and contacts are related. Both sets of figures are reported in the tables that follow.

The Colorado River. The effects of different use levels in Grand Canyon are shown in Table 2-4. The low use level, which would result in a seasonal capacity of about 4,800 people, approximates the actual use which occurred in 1968 (3,609). River contacts average one per day, and an average contact means about thirteen minutes in sight of a group of seventeen people. Contact occurs at 20 percent of all attraction sites, with little chance of meeting anyone at even popular stops like Elves' Chasm.

Table 2-4. Effects of use levels on the river experience in Grand Canyon.[a]

	Current Use Levels in People per Week			Projected Use Levels in People per Week			Correlation With Use Level
	80-400	401-700	701-950	1,000	1,250	1,500	
River Encounters							
Contacts per day	1.1	2.9	4.7	5.7	7.2	8.9	.68[*]
Minutes in sight	13	37	50	65	83	101	.47[*]
People per day	17	62	100	124	159	195	.65[*]
Percent of sites (total) with contacts	20	47	55	67	81	95	.58[*]
Attraction-site Encounters							
Probability of meeting another trip at Elves' Chasm	0	0.63	0.86	1.0	1.0	1.0	.69[*]
Average number of people met at Elves' Chasm	0	28	42	54	71	87	.43[*]

[a]These are average figures which represent ranges. They are based on current use patterns, and might change if, for example, departure schedules were altered. There are 8, 16, and 22 cases in the low, medium and high use categories, respectively.
[*]p < .01.

High use levels represent seasonal use of 16,500 people, close to actual use in 1972 (16,428). River contacts rise to almost five per day, with about fifty minutes spent in sight of other parties, and about a hundred people seen. Contact occurs at more than half of all attraction sites; the average number of people met at Elves' Chasm increases to 42.

Projected use levels indicate the consequences of increased use in the canyon. It should be pointed out that values are based on extrapolations, assuming that the linear relationships observed apply to ranges beyond these data. Actual contact levels might be higher than projected if these use levels were instituted, but they are not likely to be lower because individuals would have less flexibility to avoid contacts.

It is possible to explore the effects of still higher use levels (see Table 2-4). Use levels of 1,250 and 1,500 people per week would result in seasonal use of 25,000 and 30,000, respectively. River contacts were projected to reach seven to nine per day, and time in sight would be about an hour and a half. As many as two hundred people a day would be seen on the river. At the most popular attraction sites, encounters with large numbers of people become almost a certainty.

While experience parameters such as river and attraction site contacts in Grand Canyon increase with use levels, campsite contacts do not. The average number of camp contacts per trip is .88 at low use, .75 at medium use and .81 at high use. Camp contact rates might be affected by other management parameters such as scheduling, but they are not related to use levels. The point here is that, even in this relatively simple linear system, use level is not related to an important experience parameter. It is not always easy to demonstrate a relationship between use level and contacts, even though common sense would suggest that the two variables should always correlate.

Two factors, physical and social, work together to make camp contacts and use levels unrelated. Most beaches are out of sight and sound of each other, and floaters try to avoid camping on the same beach with another party. As long as these conditions exist, we would not expect to find increased camp contacts at higher use levels. At some point use levels might be so high that all the isolated beaches were filled every night, and then increases in use levels would mean greater camp contact. But at Grand Canyon this threshold has not yet been reached.

The kind of data specified in Table 2-4 is the *basic* information required for a carrying capacity judgment. It tells managers what happens to visitor experiences as use level increases. If use level is set at 400 per week, for example, the average floater will see one other party of seventeen people for thirteen minutes each day. There will be some variation, which is why Lime and Stankey (1971) note that carrying capacity is a probabilistic concept, but the difference between the data at low and high use levels is quite clear.

Table 2-5. Effects of use levels on the Rogue River experience.[a]

| | Current Use Level: Trips[b] and Visitors | | | | | | | |
| | Low | | Medium | | High | | Very High | |
Actual Contacts	1-4 trips	1-60 people	5-9 trips	11-90 people	10-14 trips	91-120 people	15-23 trips	120+ people
River contacts per day[1]	7.5		9.6		11.7		20.8	
Average number of people[2] per day	74		82		90		118	
Average time in sight of other parties each day in minutes[3]	77		88		121		177	

[a]Mean values.
[b]A total of five trips were in the "low" category, 14 in the medium, 8 in the high and 2 in the very high.
[1]Correlation with use level .71 (p < .01).
[2]Correlation with use level .29 (p < .01).
[3]Correlation with use level .44 (p < .01).

The Rogue River. On the lowest use days, visitors saw more than seven other groups and over seventy people on the river each day (see Table 2-5). At the highest use level, contacts increased to more than twenty parties (well over a hundred people) per day. Time in sight of other parties ranged from an hour and a quarter to almost three hours per day. As in Grand Canyon, there is a strong linear correlation between use levels and river encounters (r = .71), although a Rogue River trip involves far more contact with other groups.

Two other impact measures—attraction site contacts and camp contacts—are largely unaffected by changes in use level. For these locations, contacts are more likely to be governed by other factors, such as geographical barriers or the availability of alternative sites. Limiting encounters at these places would require other management strategies such as scheduling stops at attractions or allowing people to sign up for camps.

The Bois Brule River. As use levels go up, Brule River canoers report more encounters (see Table 2-6). On low-use days a canoer can expect to have twelve contacts, at medium use this goes up to seventeen, and at high use levels there were reports of twenty-five contacts. The same general linear relationship holds for canoer contacts with tubers and anglers. Correlations for the three types of contacts on the Brule range from .40 to .50. These are lower than the correlations between use levels and *actual* encounters found on the Colorado and the Rogue, again suggesting lowered accuracy in user reports. Even with perfect accuracy, however, one would expect these correlations to be less than 1.0 because there is natural variation in most systems. For example, a canoer could leave Stones Bridge on the busiest day of the summer and, because of an early morning departure, see only a few other canoes. Conversely, a trip could leave at a busy time on a low-use day and still run into twenty other canoes. This kind of variation reduces the one-to-one relationship between use levels and encounters.

Even though these correlations are less than perfect, they are high enough to meet the first necessary condition for establishing carrying capacity. On all three study rivers we have a known relationship between use levels (the management parameter) and contacts (the social impact). Rivers flow in only one direction, however, and most users go with the current. What happens in land-based recreation settings when people are more free to roam?

Deer hunting. Deer hunting in Wisconsin is a case where increased use does not cause an increase in encounters (see Table 2-6). In low-density management units, hunters reported an average of eight other hunters per day, in medium-density units they reported nine, and in the highest density units they reported eight. The correlation between use level and reported field contacts was -.07, which is not significantly different than zero. The implication for managers is that decreases in the numbers of hunters in certain management units would not reduce contacts on opening day, at least not within the current range of use. Just as camp encounters on the Colorado and Rogue Rivers were not related to use level, contacts between hunters in the field were not sensitive to levels of use in management units.

Table 2-6. Reported encounters at varying use levels for eight activities/locations.

Location/Activity	Use Level			Use Level-Contacts Correlations	Percent Variance Explained (r^2)
	Low	Medium	High		
Rogue River	4	4	6	.42*	18
Brule River					
Canoers	12	17	25	.46*	21
Tubers	8	13	25	.56*	31
Fishers	7	23	26	.40*	16
Wisconsin hunters					
Deer	8	9	8	-.07	0
Goose—firing line	16	25	32	.44*	19
Goose—managed hunt	3	3	3	.03	0
	4	15	27		

*p < .05 or better.

There seem to be three possible explanations for the lack of correlation:

(1) *The size of the units.* The management units are very large; most are over 500 square miles and some are more than 1,000 square miles. In all this territory there could be substantial variation from one hunting area to another. It is difficult for one hunter to cover even one-quarter of a square mile (40 acres) in a day. The aggregate use level figures for a 500 square mile unit is too broad to represent the distribution of hunters in an area where a single hunter is hunting.

(2) *Institutional constraints to hunter mobility.* In high-density units, landowners may post their land and restrict access to their own hunting party, and about 40 percent of the hunters hunt on private land. Even in a management unit with forty hunters per square mile, it is possible to see no one outside your own party. Conversely, hunters tend to congregate on public land. There may be many hunters in small public areas, even in a low- or medium-density management unit.

(3) *Purposive hunter actions.* Hunters have more freedom of movement than floaters. Some Wisconsin deer hunters believe it is necessary to have lots of people to move deer, so they seek out areas where they expect to see others. Hunters may also be attracted to good habitat areas in a low-density unit, creating high-density pockets. Conversely, hunters in high-density units may actively avoid one another, leading to lower levels of contact.

These factors combine into a complex situation. The bottom line is that a single use figure for a management unit does not adequately represent the amount of use in a given hunting area. We are continuing our deer-hunting capacity work on smaller, more homogeneous units where we expect to find a stronger relationship between use level and contact. But for managers of the state deer hunt, who can at best manage density in large management units, reductions in use levels will not reduce contacts. A capacity determination is not possible with use levels as the only management parameter.

Goose hunting. At low use levels on the firing line, hunters report contact with sixteen other hunters; this doubles at high use levels. The correlation between use levels and contacts is .44, about the same as the correlation between use levels and reported contacts on the Rogue and Brule rivers.

In contrast, the managed hunt was successful in providing low-contact hunting. It shows how the manipulation of management parameters other than use level can affect the relationship between use levels and reported encounters. Managers' efforts to disperse the blinds, screen them from one another, and restrict activity produced low contact levels, in spite of the fact that other hunters were in the area and everyone traveled on established trails. In addition, contact levels were no higher on days with thirty hunters than they were on days with thirteen. In this case, contacts do not relate to use level because other management parameters have been used to reduce the relationship between use level and encounters.

3—Evaluating Use: Satisfaction

Chapter Overview

This chapter addresses the question, "Is satisfaction useful as an evaluative standard for determining carrying capacities?" The satisfaction model comes from economics, and the implicit evaluative criterion is the point of maximum aggregate benefits. The model is based on the assumption that as use levels or encounters increase, satisfaction will decrease.

Satisfaction has been measured in some studies as hypothetical willingness to pay, in others as reported satisfaction. Studies in recreation settings, urban areas, and laboratories provide little or no support for the assumption that increases in use levels or encounters have a negative effect on satisfaction or other measures of social well-being. There are several explanations for this, including self-selection, product shifts, displacement, multiple sources of satisfaction, and rationalization.

Overall satisfaction does not seem to be a useful criterion for determining capacities. Because satisfaction is generally uncorrelated with use or encounter levels, the optimal point of maximum net benefit cannot be specified. The satisfaction concept is too general, and it is a poor indicator of user reactions to specific management decisions.

The Satisfaction Model

The previous chapter discussed the descriptive component of carrying capacity. But simply knowing the impacts associated with different levels of use will not determine a capacity. An evaluative dimension is needed to discover how people feel about different amounts of use and decide which is most desirable or appropriate. The next three chapters consider different approaches for developing evaluative standards. These chapters discuss the theoretical basis of each approach, its use by other researchers, and its usefulness for determining capacities in the areas we studied.

The satisfaction concept appears prominently in many branches of social science research. Besides investigating satisfaction derived from leisure activities, a tradition that dates back to the 1930s, researchers have explored satisfaction with marital relationships, family relationships, health care services, jobs, communities, and life in general. This work has been prolific; Gruneberg (1979), for example, estimates more than 3,000 articles and dissertations on job satisfaction alone.

The diversity of this research places a detailed review beyond the scope of this book. However, many discussions of carrying capacity involve visitor satisfaction (Wagar 1964, 1966, Lucas 1964, Lime 1977, Lucas and Stankey 1974). Lucas (1964), for example, defines "the capacity of a recreational area" as the area's ability to provide satisfaction. Similarly, Lime (1977) describes the goal of recreation management as providing "enjoyment and benefits for the people." Researchers have often argued that "the goal of recreation management is to maximize user satisfaction" (Lucas and Stankey 1974).[1]

Several economists have developed the theory and procedures for setting capacities using satisfaction as an evaluative criterion (Clawson and Knetsch 1966, Fisher and Krutilla 1972, Cicchetti and Smith 1973, 1976, Smith and Krutilla 1974). Other economists have conducted empirical research (Anderson and Bonsor 1974, McConnell 1976). The model resulting from this work is based on two assumptions: (1) the satisfaction or utility gained from a particular (in most cases wilderness) experience decreases as the number of encounters with others increases; and (2) visitors to an area react similarly to encounters (Fisher and Krutilla 1972:421-422). The usefulness of this approach depends on the empirical validity of these assumptions.

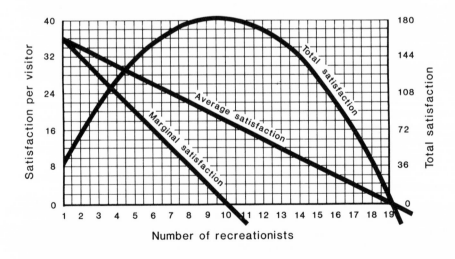

Figure 3-1. Recreation experience—the simple wilderness case.
From Alldredge 1973

Table 3-1. Recreation experience—the simple wilderness case.[*]

No. of Visitors	Per Person Enjoyment (Enjoyils)	Total Public Enjoyment	Incremental Total Enjoyment
0	0	0	0
1	36	36	36
2	34	68	32
3	32	96	28
4	30	120	24
5	28	140	20
6	26	156	16
7	24	168	12
8	22	176	8
9	20	180	4
10	18	180	0
11	16	176	−4
12	14	168	−8
13	12	156	−12
14	10	140	−16
15	8	120	−20
16	6	96	−24
17	4	68	−28
18	2	36	−32
19	0	0	−36
20	−2	−40	−40
21	−4	−84	−44

[*]From Alldredge 1973.

Alldredge (1973) describes the "economic" approach to carrying capacity in a paper that avoids the mathematical formulas found in the more abstract theoretical essays. For the sake of argument, Alldredge measures satisfaction in units he calls "enjoyils." An empty wilderness area produces no enjoyils, as shown in the first row of Table 3-1. When a single individual enters the wilderness, that person gets 36 units (an arbitrary starting-point) of enjoyment. With one individual in the area, then, the per person enjoyment is 36, total public enjoyment produced by the area is 36, and the increment in total enjoyment from adding one person to the area is 36 (see the second row of Table 3-1). Each additional visitor to the area decreases per person satisfaction by an arbitrary two enjoyils.

Adding more people increases total public satisfaction until the tenth person arrives. The introduction of the tenth visitor adds 18 enjoyils, but the decrease in solitude takes away two enjoyils from each of the other nine visitors, reducing total enjoyment by 18 units. Total public enjoyment was 180 with nine visitors, and it is 180 with ten.

In Alldredge's example carrying capacity is ten persons. This number is the optimum level based on (1) the value judgment that aggregate public benefit should be as great as possible; (2) the assumption that only one factor, use level, affects satisfaction; and (3) the assumption that increased use causes a decrease in satisfaction.

A manager who limited use to ten persons would turn away people who would have been at least partially satisfied with less than optimal conditions. Managers often confront this dilemma because they find that visitors enjoy themselves even when an area seems crowded. But the satisfaction gained by newcomers would be less than that lost by the first ten visitors.

Establishing capacity in this manner is similar to the maximum production approach in range management, where cattle are added to the herd until the beef gained from adding one more animal is just offset by the weight loss of the others. Just as a rancher can continue to add animals even though his herd will produce less meat as a result, the recreation manager can allow more visitors into an area even though total public enjoyment will be reduced.

The approach proposed by economists establishes social carrying capacity at an optimum rather than a maximum, using greatest net benefit as the evaluative standard. However, if the goal is to provide a satisfactory experience for as many people as possible, we might use a different evaluative standard and set capacity at eighteen, the highest use level at which each visitor gets at least *some* satisfaction (see Table 3-1).

Alldredge's discussion of the satisfaction model is greatly simplified. Carrying capacity researchers working with these ideas have noted that the number of contacts is probably more important than simple use level. They also point out that a variety of factors—including distribution of visitors in space and time, capital investment in facilities such as additional trails, and policies such as scheduling—could increase capacity by decreasing contacts. They also recognize that solitude is not the only factor affecting visitor satisfaction, and that wilderness recreation "has quality dimensions which include the pristine scenery, exercise, challenge of a primitive recreational experience, and a number of others" (Smith and Krutilla 1974:188). Finally the model is developed primarily for wilderness recreation in which solitude (a minimal number of contacts) is a primary criterion for evaluating quality. It is not clear how the model applies to settings where other factors have a greater effect on satisfaction.

The contribution of Alldredge's model is the development of a conceptually clear evaluative standard that preserves one dimension of quality. The evaluative standard is at least theoretically related to use levels, and it limits the numbers at some optimum rather than the maximum capacity. This is important; as Wagar (1964) points out, "Unless we consciously work toward quality, we may achieve only substandard recreation for everyone— guaranteed mediocrity!"

Empirical Tests of the Satisfaction Model

Willingness to Pay

There are two well-known tests of the economic approach. In the first of these, Cicchetti and Smith (1973, 1976) used a mailed questionnaire to present five different hypothetical situations to a sample of Spanish Peaks Wilderness visitors. Each situation involved a trip of a certain length (from one to five days), a certain number of encounters on the trail each day (between zero and three), and camping in sight of other parties a certain number of nights (from zero to four). For each hypothetical trip, respondents were asked to indicate the highest price they would be willing to pay (as an indicator of satisfaction).

The response rate to the survey was low. With one follow-up reminder, less than 50 percent returned the questionnaire, and of those who did, only two-thirds (195 of the original 600 surveyed) answered the willingness-to-pay questions (Cicchetti and Smith 1973, footnote 18). In mailed surveys of wilderness visitors, response rates of 70 percent or better are common (Lucas and Oltman 1971). The low response rate reported by Cicchetti and Smith may indicate that respondents had difficulty with the hypothetical scenarios, the willingness-to-pay measure, or both.

Initially, the Cicchetti and Smith study showed *no* relationship between encounters and willingness to pay. The zero order correlation between willingness to pay and trail encounters with backpackers was -.05, and even for encounters with horse parties the correlation was -.06. For camp encounters the correlations were .00 and -.01, respectively. None of these correlations is significantly different than zero; people were not willing to pay more for lower levels of hypothetical contact.

Cicchetti and Smith then looked at the other variables available on the questionnaire. They found that men, those with longer vacations, those with higher incomes, and those who were presented with longer trips were willing to pay more. After these four variables were controlled statistically, the number of campsite and trail contacts *did* reduce willingness to pay slightly. Even taken together, however, these six variables explained only 5 percent of the variance in willingness to pay.

Cicchetti and Smith went on to estimate optimum use levels for the Spanish Peaks area using techniques developed by Fisher and Krutilla (1972) and described by Alldredge (1973). They concluded that a daily use level of 150 would produce three trail encounters per day, 2.25 camp encounters per trip, and $13,650 of net benefits. If use increased to 200, trail contacts would increase to four a day, and camp encounters to three per trip, and net benefits would reach a maximum of $14,170. If use increased to 350 a day, trail encounters would rise to five per day, and camp encounters to 3.75 per trip, and net benefits would drop to $11,970.

It appears that capacity has been established at approximately 200 visitors per day. But because of the complexity of the hypothetical scenarios and the low response rate, the authors conclude, "It should be clear that this example has no direct implication for the Spanish Peaks Area" (1976:76).

A second test of the economic approach was conducted by McConnell (1976). His research team visited six Rhode Island ocean beaches, recorded the air temperature and number of people per acre on the beach, and then interviewed visitors to measure willingness to pay and other variables. Respondents were asked whether or not they would come to the beach on that particular day as the hypothetical price was increased in fifty cent increments. The highest amount a person would pay was the willingness-to-pay measure.

With data aggregated across all six beaches, there was no significant bivariate correlation between density and willingness to pay ($r = .04$). However, people were willing to pay more on warmer days ($r = .21$) and less if they visited the beach frequently ($r = .44$). Controlling for these two variables and income (which did not have a significant effect), the partial correlation between density and willingness to pay increased to .21 ($p < .01$). Using the maximum benefits criterion, McConnell went on to estimate capacity at 400 people per acre on ocean beaches; he pointed out that official Bureau of Outdoor Recreation standards of 580 people per acre may be too high.

In general, McConnell's findings are more credible than the Cicchetti and Smith study because they are based on a field study. However, there are two complicating factors. The first involves statistical control, which was also an issue in the Cicchetti and Smith study. Capacities are based on the relationship between density and willingness to pay after controlling for income, air temperature, and visits per season, all factors which vary naturally. The intention, of course, is to isolate the effect of density from the extraneous variables in a system, a reasonable goal from a scientific point of view. But real-life attempts to set use limits will have to contend with other variables.

In McConnell's study, capacity would be higher on hotter days or when there was a lower proportion of frequent visitors. It seems unlikely, however, that managers would find it practical to limit use at one level on cool days and at a higher level on hot days. The same point applies to Cicchetti and Smith's work in the Spanish Peaks, where capacity would increase when there were higher proportions of men, people with higher incomes, and people with longer vacations.

For applications to resource areas, the variables entered into the equation for determining capacity should be limited to those which managers can actually control or hold constant. Because none of the control variables considered in the two economic studies discussed above can be controlled by managers, the bivariate relationships between density and willingness to pay should be used for setting limits. *Because these bivariate relationships are essentially zero, no capacity can be established using maximum net benefits as an evaluative standard.*

McConnell's work illustrates a second complication with capacity determination. The beaches he studied varied considerably. They included an undeveloped beach near a wildlife refuge, a "singles" beach, and a highly developed beach with an eating stand, shower facilities, and cabanas. Results showed that the relationship between density and willingness to pay was different on the different beaches. With the same procedure used to develop the 400 person per acre average, McConnell went on to calculate capacities for each beach separately. Estimates were 28 people per acre for the wildlife beach, 2,127 per acre for the singles beach, and 5,090 per acre (about 8 square feet per person) for the highly developed beach. Obviously social aspects of the experience desired have an important impact, and carrying capacities must be established separately for different kinds of experiences.

Satisfaction as an Alternative to Willingness to Pay

The use of hypothetical willingness to pay as the measure of satisfaction may be one of the reasons for the disappointing results in these studies. Fisher and Krutilla (1972) and Cicchetti and Smith (1973, 1976) have pointed out several problems with this approach. First, people may be motivated to understate their willingness to pay for something which they currently enjoy at little or no charge. If someone discovers you are *willing* to pay more for something, you might *actually* have to pay the higher price some time. Second, individuals confronted with a hypothetical situation may not act as they would in a real situation. Saying you would pay $20 for something may be easier than actually parting with a $20 bill, as the "talk is cheap" adage suggests. In a study conducted in Wisconsin (Bishop and Heberlein 1979), real dollars and hypothetical dollars had quite different effects on value estimates. Third, because income is not evenly distributed, an individual who places a high value on something like wilderness recreation may not have the money to pay for it; ability to pay may affect willingness to pay. Finally, many benefits—solitude, for example—are hard to define in monetary terms.

Fisher and Krutilla (1972:421) argue that "benefits" refer to "the satisfaction or utility gained from the wilderness experience." Overall satisfaction based on user reports avoids some of the methodological problems of willingness to pay. First, the question of satisfaction is not hypothetical; recreationists feel some degree of satisfaction which they can readily report. Second, there is no motivation to overstate or understate satisfaction because it is not related to user fees. Third, visitors do not have to convert their enjoyment or benefits into dollars. Fourth, the problem of unequal distribution is avoided.

This approach has some disadvantages. If one simply asks people if they are satisfied with a recreation experience, almost everyone will say "yes" (Heberlein and Shelby 1977), so it is important to measure gradations in satisfaction. The following satisfaction measure was used in our studies:

Overall, how would you rate your trip?

_____ Poor
_____ Fair, it just didn't work out very well
_____ Good, but I wish a number of things could have been different
_____ Very good, but could have been better
_____ Excellent, only minor problems
_____ Perfect

A set of items combined into a scale will usually measure psychological constructs more reliably than a single item, but a single item is easier to use. It easily fits into a short questionnaire which can be given in a field setting, responses are more meaningful intuitively, and it is easier to compare across studies. Ditton et al. (1979) measured various dimensions of satisfaction among Buffalo River floaters. They found that a single general item such as the one above worked about as well as multiple item scales. For these reasons, this appears to be a better measure of user benefits than hypothetical willingness to pay.

The satisfaction levels observed in our studies are shown graphically in Table 3-2 and in more quantitative detail in Table 3-3. They show considerable variation between sites and activities. Rogue River floaters were the most satisfied; 90 percent rated their trip excellent or perfect. Grand Canyon floaters were next, with 84 percent reporting this same level of satisfaction. Brule River floaters had lower levels of satisfaction; 65 percent of the tubers and 67 percent of the canoers rated their trip as excellent or perfect.

The hunters and fishers reported much lower levels of satisfaction. Only 9 percent of the firing line goose hunters gave excellent or perfect ratings, and this group was the least satisfied of the nine types of recreationists studied. The differences between satisfaction levels of the hunters and fishers and those of river recreationists are more systematically explored in Vaske et al. (1982).

Use Levels, Encounters, and Satisfaction

Use Levels and Satisfaction

If the satisfaction model proposed by Alldredge (1973) and others is to be used for determining carrying capacity, satisfaction must decrease with increasing levels of use. As discussed earlier, this negative relationship should exist when no other variables are controlled statistically. Cicchetti and Smith (1973) and McConnell (1977) did not find this relationship in their data.

Table 3-2. Ranked satisfaction ratings.

```
Percent Indicating
Excellent or Perfect
        100
         95
         90 — Rogue River floaters
         85
         80 — Grand Canyon floaters
         75
         70 — Brule River canoers
         65 — Brule River tubers
         60
         55
         50
         45
         40
         35 — Brule River fishers
         30 — Goose hunters—managed hunt
         25 — Goose hunters—Horicon
         20 — Wisconsin deer hunters
         15
         10
          5 — Goose hunters—firing line
          0
```

Table 3-3. Frequency distributions for satisfaction.

Location/Activity	Percent Rating Trip As			Sample Size
	Poor/Fair	Good/ Very Good	Excellent/Perfect	
Grand Canyon[a]	1	15	84	984
Rogue River	0	9	90	339
Brule River				
Canoers	4	30	67	2,218
Tubers	5	31	65	480
Fishers	22	44	35	164
Wisconsin hunters				
Deer	25	51	25	234
Goose (firing line)[b]	69	22	9	442
Goose (managed hunt)[b]	45	22	33	909

[a]Poor category not on scale.
[b]Very good category not on scale.

Empirical relationships found in our study areas are presented in Table 3-4. In the Grand Canyon, visitors were just as satisfied at high use levels as they were at lower use levels. On the Rogue River, 91 percent were satisfied at low use levels, as were 90 percent when use was three times as high. Again, the correlation between use level and satisfaction was zero. The same was true for Brule River canoers, tubers, and anglers, and for the two goose hunter samples; at low use levels visitors were not significantly more satisfied than they were at high use levels. Only among deer hunters did use levels affect satisfaction—but these deer hunters were *more*, rather than *less*, satisfied at higher use levels. In eight separate surveys reported in Table 3-4, the required relationship between satisfaction and use level was not observed.

Encounters and Satisfaction

If a relationship between satisfaction and contacts (encounters) could be identified and if use levels and contacts were related, an approximation of the economic model could be used to establish social carrying capacity. The relationship between encounters and satisfaction is reported in Table 3-5. The findings closely parallel the findings on use level and satisfaction reported in Table 3-4. Grand Canyon visitors, Rogue River visitors, Brule River fishers, and Wisconsin goose hunters felt no less satisfied when encounters with other recreationists increased.

For six out of nine cases data do not support the negative relationship between contacts and satisfaction. Among the three negatively affected groups of recreationists only the Brule River canoers showed a statistically

Table 3-4. Use levels and satisfaction.

Area	Percent Satisfied[a] at			Use Level- Satisfaction Correlations[b]
	Low Use	Medium Use	High Use	
Grand Canyon	85.4	83.2	85.1	−.00
Rogue River	90.9	90.1	89.5	−.00
Brule River				
Canoers	68.9	72.4	65.4	−.06
Tubers	57.2	69.8	65.9	.00
Fishers	23.7	25.7	34.1	.11
Wisconsin hunters				
Deer	21.7	22.5	36.4	.17[*]
Goose (firing line)	12.1	9.8	4.2	.01
Goose (managed hunt)	32.7	28.9	36.5	.02

[a]Those rating their trip as "excellent" or "perfect."
[b]Use level break points for each area are described in Table 2-1.
[*]p < .001.

significant relationship, although the correlation was low. The relationship between contacts and satisfaction for tubers was higher, but was not statistically significant because of the smaller sample size. Deer hunters also showed a slight, although nonsignificant, relationship of about the same magnitude.

To summarize, the procedures for using satisfaction as an evaluative standard have been worked out theoretically. But empirical tests by economists show that the necessary relationship does not exist without statistical controls. In addition, use level was not related to satisfaction in any of our own studies, and encounters were not significantly correlated with satisfaction in eight of the nine situations. In general, the basic assumption of the satisfaction model is not supported by our data.

Evidence from Other Studies

Sociologists and social psychologists have explored the effects of density and crowding in many contexts, but most studies show little or no relationship between these variables and various evaluative criteria. Schmitt (1966), Winsborough (1965), and Galle et al. (1972) investigated urban census tracts to see how density affects social impact measures such as mental illness, crime rates, welfare payments, infant death rates, and so on. High-density neighborhoods tend to have higher rates of these social maladies, but residents are also more likely to be poor; once the effect of income is

Table 3-5. Encounters and satisfaction.

| Area | Percent Satisfied[a] at | | | Use Level-Satisfaction Correlations |
	Low Contact	Medium Contact	High Contact	
Grand Canyon (actual)	82.2	85.5	85.9	.05
Rogue River (reported)	86.0	92.5	87.7	.02
Rogue River (actual)	87.6	86.5	97.1	.06
Brule River				
Canoers	72.4	68.8	61.7	−.11*
Tubers	66.7	65.3	64.0	−.15
Fishers	24.1	35.7	28.6	.08
Wisconsin hunters				
Deer	31.0	25.4	18.6	−.10
Goose (firing line)	9.4	7.7	8.3	.06
Goose (managed hunt)	30.4	34.4	36.5	.05

[a]Those rating their trip as "excellent" or "perfect".
*The figure for Brule canoers is significantly different than zero (p < .05); none of the other correlations reach statistical significance.

taken into account, density has little or no effect. Higher density in cities seems to have little negative social impact independent of income and social class.

In a nationwide survey, Baldassare (1978) found no effect of neighborhood density ($r = -.06$) or household density ($r = -.06$) on how satisfied individuals were with their life as a whole. All over the United States, people who live in higher density neighborhoods and in households with more than the average number of people per room report that they are just as satisfied with life as those who live in more spacious surroundings.

Density can be carefully manipulated in more controlled laboratory conditions, but social psychologists have found little evidence of negative effects due to high density. Early studies reviewed by Freedman (1975) showed no clear effects of density on performance, and neither do more recent studies (Stockdale 1978).

Satisfaction is a common dependent variable in studies of communities, marriages, and jobs. Researchers in these areas indicate that satisfaction is determined by a number of diverse factors (Campbell et al. 1976). Variables can be categorized as describing objective characteristics (such as doctors or hospitals *per capita* in a community) and subjective evaluations (such as perceived adequacy of medical care). Objective characteristics explain little or no variation in satisfaction, while subjective evaluations explain 10-40 percent (see Shelby et al. 1980). Density levels and numbers of contacts are types of objective characteristics; based on these earlier findings, one would not expect high correlations with satisfaction.

Other recreation studies also show little relationship between use level and satisfaction. In a comprehensive review of the literature, Kuss et al. (1984) found fourteen studies reporting relationships between density and satisfaction. Of these, twelve showed no significant correlation. The two significant relationships were both positive (increased density was associated with increased satisfaction), the opposite direction from that predicted by the satisfaction model. There were twenty-three studies reporting correlations between encounters and satisfaction. Of these, twenty were not significant, two were significant and positive ($r = .18$ and $.23$), and only one was in the direction predicted by the satisfaction model (significant and negative, $r = -.11$).

The only exception to this string of consistently negative evidence comes from data collected by Lucas (1980) between 1970 and 1972 in nine Forest Service Wilderness Areas. His questionnaire contained a five-point satisfaction measure and an open-ended measure of reported contacts. In seven of the nine areas, the relationship between these two measures was statistically significant. Reported contacts explained between 8 and 31 percent of the variance in satisfaction across samples. This suggests that there may be some circumstances where satisfaction is related to reported contacts. This area warrants further research.

In summary, the lack of relationship between use level or contacts and satisfaction found in the two economic studies and in most of our data is generally consistent with other evidence. Sociological studies usually find little or no effect of density on social impact measures, psychological studies show few major effects in more controlled laboratory settings, and national surveys of satisfaction produce the same result. Generally, the literature shows that objective conditions such as density have little effect on satisfaction. Research in a variety of recreation settings shows no relationship in most cases. Lucas's work suggests that there may be circumstances when reported contact does influence satisfaction, and further research to identify these conditions would be useful. But the evidence suggests that the basic assumption of the satisfaction model is untenable.

Why Use Levels and Contacts Do Not Affect Satisfaction

It seems counterintuitive that satisfaction does not drop as use levels and contacts increase. But careful social-scientific inquiry often challenges untested assumptions. Possible explanations for the lack of relationship are discussed in the remainder of this chapter.

Self-Selection

People may do things they don't enjoy in other areas of their lives, but recreation usually involves free choice. There may be some constraints (going to a movie your spouse wants to see, for example), but generally people choose recreation activities they enjoy and avoid those they do not. Assuming that visitors' expectations are realistic, we would expect high levels of satisfaction, regardless of use level, simply because people select experiences they will enjoy.

Product Shifts

Economists are careful to limit their model of carrying capacity to a particular kind of experience. But what exactly is the product of a recreation experience? Consumers are not likely to buy a car when they want a truck or an apple when they want a grapefruit. These products are clearly different, and not clearly confused. But in a recreation setting the "product" is often more difficult to specify; it exists largely in the mind of the user.

For example, you might start a hike down the Bright Angel Trail in the Grand Canyon expecting a wilderness experience, a product with certain attributes including few encounters with others. As you meet more and more people, you have two choices other than actually leaving the situation: you can be dissatisfied, or you can reevaluate the experience. In the latter case, you might say to yourself, "There are a lot of hikers here, the trail is wide and heavily trampled, and many people are dressed in street clothes. Maybe this isn't a place for a wilderness experience after all."

You may define the new experience as "hiking on a developed trail." It is now appropriate to use a different yardstick to evaluate the number of contacts. Five per day may be too many for a wilderness experience, and if you got this recreation product you would be dissatisfied. But five contacts a day may be low for hiking on a developed trail, so you are not dissatisfied. You just needed to change your mind about the product you are getting.

This example suggests that users may change their definitions of recreation experiences to cope with excessive encounter levels. As a result, they may remain satisfied as contacts increase. In addition, the contacts them-

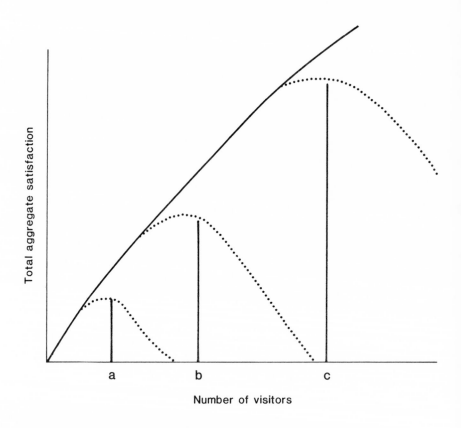

Number of visitors

Figure 3-2. Hypothesized diagram of product shift.
Points *a, b,* and *c* show social carrying capacities for wilderness, semi-wilderness, and more developed recreation settings, respectively. A new curve describes the hypothetical use level-satisfaction relationship as the product (the recreation experience) shifts. The solid line shows the observed relationship if product shift is not taken into account.

selves may play a role in changing the definition of the situation. One way hikers know they are in a wilderness is that they see few other people. Seeing more people than anticipated may change the definition of a situation and the corresponding evaluative standards. Different products imply more users, higher acceptable use or encounter levels, and higher aggregate satisfaction, as Figure 3-2 suggests.

The product shift hypothesis has been proposed by Hendee et al. (1978:178), but it is speculative and needs empirical testing. Limited data from the Rogue River provide some support for the hypothesis. Floaters were asked what they did when they met more parties than they had expected. They were given three behavioral options (speed up or slow down, change stops or camps, or decide to go somewhere else next time) and two psychological ones (become dissatisfied with the trip, or change the way they thought about the Rogue). Very few became dissatisfied, while 30-40 percent said they changed their perception of the Rogue and/or engaged in the behavioral options. This is consistent with the notion of a product shift, but more evidence is needed.

Displacement

Product shift and self-selection together form the basis for a third explanation of the lack of relationship between use level and satisfaction. As use increases and capacities are exceeded, the kind of experience available changes. Dissatisfied users may leave the area in search of lower-density experiences more desirable to them, being replaced by those less sensitive to high density. A cross-sectional study of an area might show a high level of satisfaction in spite of crowding problems because density-sensitive users would not be represented in the user population. Finding this displaced group would require longitudinal studies (which follow the same population over time) or regional studies (which examine users in settings with different density levels). Because such studies are difficult, there is little evidence of the self-selection/displacement process. Findings from the few published empirical studies (Nielsen and Endo 1977, Becker et al. 1979) do not have the longitudinal data for a convincing test of the hypothesis. We found that more experienced visitors to the Apostle Islands sought out areas with lower densities to avoid crowds (Vaske et al. 1980).

The displacement hypothesis also assumes that acceptable substitutions are available. Limited evidence suggests there are few substitutes for river trips through the Grand Canyon, for example (Dekker 1976). In such cases people would probably continue to visit the area but complain more, learn to maximize the satisfactions gained from other aspects of the experience, or make the cognitive adjustments involved in a product shift, rather than stop visiting the area and not replace the experience. All these mechanisms would counteract the displacement phenomenon. We do not have the data needed to explore these issues.

Multiple Sources of Satisfaction

Satisfaction is a broad psychological construct; the number of other people is only one of many things that might affect it. The recreation literature has many references to the "multiple satisfactions" derived from experiences. Even in wilderness recreation, where solitude is important, people get satisfaction from being close to nature, being with friends and family, the physical effort involved, and so on. As a result, a satisfying recreation experience may occur even when use levels are high. Conversely, you can have a miserable time in spite of minimal contact if it rains on your leaky tent or you destroy your boat by tipping over in a rapid.

It is possible to measure these other aspects of the recreation experience to see how they influence satisfaction. Table 3-6 shows data for Grand Canyon visitors. The first variables listed are density and interaction measures. None showed a significant effect on satisfaction, and together they explain less than 1.5 percent of the variance in the overall trip rating.

Personal benefits such as learning and personal growth explained about 10 percent of the variance in satisfaction. Social aspects of the trip, such as getting along with others in the group or having a good boatman, also had a major effect, adding another 14 percent to the explained variance. Because the canyon offers a wilderness setting, those who sought this opportunity and felt the experience fit this definition were more satisfied, as were those who were prepared for the trip and had better weather. These nondensity variables explain over 30 percent of the variance in satisfaction, while use level and contact variables explain less than 1.5 percent. If you don't like the people on your trip, have a sour boatman, don't learn much, don't like wilderness, or are unprepared for the trip, you will probably be less satisfied with a trip on the Colorado River.

A study of Wisconsin deer hunters (Heberlein and Laybourne 1978) shows similar results. Both the 1976 and 1977 surveys showed three important predictors of satisfaction. Hunters who saw more deer, got more shooting, and actually bagged a deer were more likely to be satisfied. Taken together, these three variables accounted for 24 percent of the variance in satisfaction in 1976 and 17 percent in 1977, while density and contact explained almost none of the variance. This may explain why hunters in high-density units are more satisfied than those in less crowded areas, where deer may be less abundant and there is less opportunity for shooting.

Rationalizing

Most recreationists are out to have fun, and have fun they will. This means they are likely to make the best of even a bad situation, focusing on positive aspects and minimizing those that are less pleasant. People say things such as: "Remember the trip when it stormed so hard the first night? The tent got ripped so we had to improvise a shelter, and everything was so wet we spent the next day standing around the fire drying out?" People in

Table 3-6. Effects of crowding and noncrowding variables on satisfaction on Colorado River (overall trip rating).

Variable	Correlation With Satisfaction[a]	Total R^2 (Cumulative)
Density and Interaction		
People per week leaving Lee's Ferry	.00	
River contacts per day	.05	
People per day seen on river	.03	
Time in sight of other people on river	.10[*]	
Percent of attraction sites with contact	−.01	
Average number people seen at attraction sites	.02	
Multiple correlation	.18	.014[*]
Personal Benefits		
Learning	.31[*]	
Personal growth	.19[*]	
Multiple correlation	.32[*]	.107[*]
Social Aspects		
High quality group experience	.32[*]	
Accessibility of boatmen	.32[*]	
High rating of boatmen	.37[*]	
Unambiguous passenger role	.28[*]	
Multiple correlation	.49[*]	.249[*]
Character of Wilderness Experience		
Being in wilderness an important reason for trip	.20[*]	
Pace of trip perceived as leisurely	.29[*]	
Trip evaluated as "nature experience"	.31[*]	
Trip perceived as "noisy"	−.24[*]	
Use impact perceived as high	−.20[*]	
More conveniences preferred	−.29[*]	
Multiple correlation	.47	.302[*]
Weather and Preparation		
Weather perceived as bad	−.22[*]	
Was unprepared for trip	−.22[*]	
Multiple correlation	−.32[*]	.319[*]

[a]Multiple correlation in the left column shows the relationship between satisfaction and variables in a particular group. Total R^2 in right column is cumulative for all variables.
[*]$p < .01$.

recreation situations seem to have a good time under sometimes awful conditions, perhaps in defiance of conventional rationality. People who complain about the number of others on a river are still likely to have a good time, and by the end of the trip they may have learned to ignore the negative aspects of seeing other groups to capitalize on positive aspects such as sharing information or food. Contacts can thus become a less important part of the total experience.

Table 3-7. Perceived crowding and satisfaction.

	Percent Satisfied[a] at			Perceived Crowding/ Satisfaction Correlation	R²
	Low Crowding	Medium Crowding	High Crowding		
Grand Canyon	86.7	84.2	79.2	−.14[*]	.02
Rogue River	97.4	86.2	85.7	−.15[*]	.02
Brule River					
Canoers	71.7	62.1	57.1	−.15	.02
Tubers	68.8	60.3	....	−.12	.01
Fishers	29.3	30.6	10.0	−.01	.00
Wisconsin hunters					
Deer	35.1	18.0	0.0	−.18	.03
Goose (firing line)	13.3	9.8	4.9	−.03	.00
Goose (managed hunt)	35.5	20.3	11.1	−.11[*]	.01

[a]Those rating their trip as excellent or perfect experiences.
[b]A crowding scale was used here (see Shelby 1970).
[*]p < .05.

Crowding and Satisfaction

Crowding is a negative evaluation of a particular number of people (to be discussed further in Chapter 4). Considering the many things affecting satisfaction with recreation experiences, we would expect the effect of crowding alone to be small. Hunters who bag deer will probably be satisfied even if they felt crowded, as will the well-prepared rafter with a good crew.

The relationship between crowding and satisfaction is shown in Table 3-7. In all but one case, there is a statistically significant relationship, meaning that people who felt crowded tended to be less satisfied. But the correlations are quite small, ranging from .10 to .20; perceived crowding accounts for only 1-4 percent of the variance in satisfaction. Taken together the other measured characteristics of a Grand Canyon trip have fifteen times more influence on satisfaction. Crowding plays a demonstrable but small role in satisfaction with recreation experiences.

Conclusion

This chapter shows that the assumptions of the satisfaction model are not supported by empirical evidence. Studies in recreation settings, urban areas, and laboratories show that use levels and encounters have little effect on satisfaction. In addition, many factors other than contacts, use level, or even perceived crowding have a big influence on satisfaction.

People are equally satisfied at both low and high use levels. Does this mean managers should forget about carrying capacity? We think not. In the areas we studied many people complained about crowding and insisted that capacity had been exceeded, even though satisfaction levels were sometimes quite high. Encounters may play a relatively small part in the overall satisfaction of users, but it seems likely that the presence of an endangered species or the erosion of stream banks has an equally small impact on satisfaction. Yet all these things are important aspects of resource management and deserve the attention of managers. A more precise tool than satisfaction is needed to determine carrying capacity.

Managers of recreation resources are generally committed to providing opportunities for certain kinds of experiences; recreationists are then free to choose what they want. The goal of management is not to increase satisfaction *per se*, but rather to provide a satisfactory experience of a certain type. Hotels, showers, indoor plumbing, bars, and tennis courts might increase satisfaction at the bottom of the Grand Canyon, for example. But they would greatly change the wilderness character of river experiences, and for that reason they would be out of place. Focusing on satisfaction alone blinds us to these issues.

Notes

1. The satisfaction concept applies to recreation management in two other ways, although neither has been used extensively in carrying capacity research. A popular approach among recreation researchers considers the satisfaction of human needs as the primary benefit of recreation (Wagar 1966, Hendee 1974, Dorfman 1979, Driver and Knopf 1977, Tinsley and Kass 1978). As Wagar (1955:10) explains, "The quality of recreation depends on how well it satisfies the needs that motivate it. An experience that thoroughly satisfies many needs will have higher quality than an experience that only satisfies a few needs." This statement implies an evaluative standard for carrying capacities; if one level of contact better satisfies needs, then it is more desirable. The procedures for using this approach to establish carrying capacity have not been developed, although need satisfaction and the perception of crowding have been studied by Schreyer and Roggenbuck (1978).

A second approach to satisfaction involves a concept called "satisficing." The idea is that people cope with uncertainty by looking for satisfactory solutions rather than optimal ones; they engage in "satisficing" rather than "optimizing" behavior. Herbert Simon applies this term to the behavior of business firms (Simon 1956), and geographers have found it useful for explaining human responses to natural hazards such as floods or earthquakes (Slovic et al. 1974). In recreation management it often seems that visitors expect, and managers try to provide, a satisfactory rather than an optimal experience.

4—Evaluating Use: Feeling Crowded

Chapter Overview

Density is an objective measure of the number of people per unit area, while perceived crowding is a negative evaluation of a particular density level in a particular setting. Crowding, then, is both subjective and situation-specific.

There are at least two ways that perceived crowding can be used to approximate an evaluative standard. The first simply assesses the percentage of visitors who feel crowded. Data comparing twenty-two different study groups suggest that capacity has probably been exceeded if more than two-thirds of the visitors feel crowded. If fewer than one-third feel crowded, the area is probably below carrying capacity, although increases in use should be made with caution. When perceived crowding is between these two thresholds, no determination can be made with this standard. A second standard involves break points, where large increases in perceived crowding occur at certain use or contact levels. Break points were found in fewer than half the cases studied here.

Finally, perceived crowding is related to a number of social psychological factors. In most cases these factors have a greater impact on crowding perceptions than use levels or encounters, so the evaluative criterion depends primarily on factors beyond the control of management. As a result, the social carrying capacity of an area would change as the user population, their expectations, or their preferences changed. As an evaluative standard, perceived crowding is more specific and therefore more useful than satisfaction. But there are still sufficient problems to suggest that this is not the optimum solution.

Feeling Crowded

Crowding refers specifically to numbers of people, so it is at least potentially a better evaluative standard than satisfaction. When there are too many people in a recreation setting, the situation is described by users and managers as "crowded" or even as "overcrowded."[1] Crowding is defined as a negative evaluation of a certain density or number of encounters (Desor 1972, Stokols 1972a, Altman 1975, Schmidt and Keating 1979).

There is a difference between density and crowding. Most theorists recognize this (Desor 1972, Stokols 1972a, 1972b, Lawrence 1974, Altman 1975, Rappoport 1975, Stockdale 1978), but even scientists (e.g., Galle et al. 1972, Langer and Saegert 1977) sometimes use the word "crowding" inappropriately when they really mean high density. Density is a descriptive term which refers to the number of people per unit area. It is measured by counting the number of people and measuring the space they occupy, and it can be determined objectively. Crowding, on the other hand, is a negative *evaluation* of density; it involves a value judgment that the specified number is too many. The term "perceived crowding" is often used to emphasize the subjective or evaluative nature of the concept.

An example may help to clarify these terms. Suppose there are ten people in a room one day and a hundred the next. Clearly density is higher the second day, but is the room more crowded? If the room is a convention hall, even a hundred people is not a crowd, so it would be uncrowded both days.[2] If it were a small office it might be crowded both times. Density is objective, but crowding involves a value judgment requiring information about the setting, the desired activity, and the individual making the evaluation. For purposes of clarity, the term "crowd" should not be substituted for high density or large numbers. Doing so confuses the objective *impacts* of larger numbers of people with the subjective *evaluation* of those impacts.

Theoretically, use level influences contacts, while contacts influence perceived crowding. If these relationships hold, it would be possible to determine the use and encounter levels which produce a certain level of perceived crowding. Social carrying capacity could then be established if there were an evaluative standard specifying the appropriate level of perceived crowding. This chapter will examine the relationships between use level, contacts, and perceived crowding and explore possible ways to use perceived crowding as an evaluative standard.[3]

Measuring Perceived Crowding

Perceived crowding is a psychological dimension which exists in the minds of individuals; it is usually measured directly by self-report techniques. For most of our studies, crowding was measured by simply asking people how crowded they felt. Responses were given on the scale shown below.

1	2	3	4	5	6	7	8	9
	Not at all crowded		Slightly crowded		Moderately crowded		Extremely crowded	

In this item, seven of the nine scale points label the situation as crowded to some degree. The rationale is that people may be reluctant to say an area was crowded because crowding is an undesirable characteristic in a recreation setting. An item which asked "Did you feel crowded?" might lead most people to say, "No," because those who felt a little crowded would be reluctant to say yes to such a blunt question. The scale needs to be sensitive enough to pick up even slight degrees of perceived crowding.[4]

Percent Feeling Crowded as an Evaluative Standard

Suppose there are one hundred people in an area. If ninety-nine feel "not at all crowded" and one feels "slightly crowded," social carrying capacity probably has not been reached. If everyone feels "extremely crowded," however, capacity probably has been exceeded. We need some way to determine the point in between where perceptions of crowdedness move from acceptable to unacceptable levels.

We have used the single item crowding measure to survey twenty-two recreation populations, including the six populations discussed in this book. Visitor density in these settings varied greatly; some had abnormally high densities, while others were managed for unusually low densities. When viewed in the context of a number of studies, responses to this single crowding question may provide a simple way to see whether a problem exists and to determine the need for further research.

Table 4-1 ranks the crowding perceptions (the percent reporting some degree of crowding, scale points 3-9) for the different areas. They break into three distinct groups. The most crowded settings, where over two-thirds feel crowded, are three hunting areas. The Bong recreation area is in southeastern Wisconsin near three major population centers. While it is a large area of about 4,000 acres, there are more than 1,700 hunters on opening day, so each hunter has less than three acres to himself. The "control" areas near Bong also have very high densities, and most managers and many hunters feel that hunter numbers on opening day exceed carrying capacity for pheasant hunting. The goose hunting firing line has been discussed in detail and, like the Bong area on opening day, it is an extreme case of high density.

Three other areas also show high levels of crowding. Rogue River floaters have considerably higher contact levels than Colorado River floaters, and other data suggest that use on the Rogue exceeds social carrying capacity (as we will show in the next chapter). We have less information about the canoers and boaters in the Boundary Waters Canoe Area, but the national focus on crowding issues suggests this is a problem area. As the highest point in North America, Mt. McKinley attracts climbers from all over the world. Over 90 percent of them report seeing human waste and discarded refuse from other groups. Almost all parties see and camp near other climbers, and 33 percent reported direct interference from others. As a result, 70 percent felt crowded.

At the other end of the scale are three areas where use was restricted or densities were lower than normal. The managed goose hunt, which was designed to limit density and encounters (as described in Chapter 2), had

Table 4-1. Ranking of perceived crowding for different settings and activities.

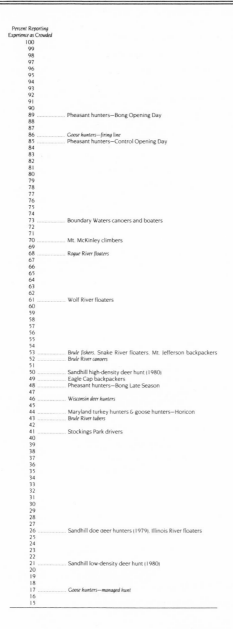

Percent Reporting Experience as Crowded	
100	
99	
98	
97	
96	
95	
94	
93	
92	
91	
90	
89	.... Pheasant hunters—Bong Opening Day
88	
87	
86	.... *Goose hunters—firing line*
85	.... Pheasant hunters—Control Opening Day
84	
83	
82	
81	
80	
79	
78	
77	
76	
75	
74	
73	.... Boundary Waters canoers and boaters
72	
71	
70	.... Mt. McKinley climbers
69	
68	.... *Rogue River floaters*
67	
66	
65	
64	
63	
62	
61	.... Wolf River floaters
60	
59	
58	
57	
56	
55	
54	
53	.... *Brule fishers,* Snake River floaters, Mt. Jefferson backpackers
52	.... *Brule River canoers*
51	
50	.... Sandhill high-density deer hunt (1980)
49	.... Eagle Cap backpackers
48	.... Pheasant hunters—Bong Late Season
47	
46	.... *Wisconsin deer hunters*
45	
44	.... Maryland turkey hunters & goose hunters—Horicon
43	.... *Brule River tubers*
42	
41	.... Stockings Park drivers
40	
39	
38	
37	
36	
35	
34	
33	
32	
31	
30	
29	
28	
27	
26	.... Sandhill doe deer hunters (1979), Illinois River floaters
25	
24	
23	
22	
21	.... Sandhill low-density deer hunt (1980)
20	
19	
18	
17	.... *Goose hunters—managed hunt*
16	
15	

the lowest level of perceived crowding. The Sandhill Wildlife Area is a controlled 12-square-mile hunting area in central Wisconsin. Hunter density was limited to twelve hunters per square mile, although the statewide average is about twenty-five per square mile. In 1979 26 percent felt crowded, and in 1980 21 percent felt crowded. This is an interesting contrast to a 1980 test area in one quadrant of Sandhill where density was increased to twenty-five hunters per square mile; here 50 percent of the hunters felt crowded. The Illinois River in Oregon was selected for study because it had not yet been discovered by large numbers of river runners, and managers wanted to get baseline data before the area became crowded. Most floaters had less than one contact per day, and only 26 percent felt crowded.

These data suggest that responses to the perceived crowding item can be used as a rough evaluative standard, at least for the high and low ends of the scale. A manager or researcher can survey visitors and then compare

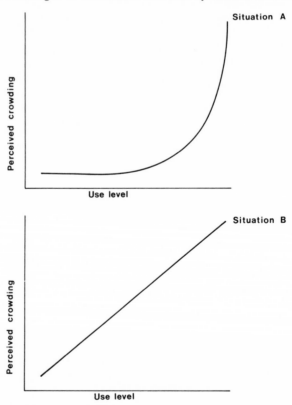

Figure 4-1. Break points as evaluative standards.

the results with Table 4-1. If more than two-thirds say they are crowded, it appears likely that capacity has been exceeded. Use limits should be considered, although further study would be needed to specify capacity. If less than one-third of the visitors feel crowded, use levels are probably below capacity. The area may bear further watching if use is increasing, but crowding probably is not yet a major issue. For areas falling between one-third and two-thirds, no clear judgment can be made and more data should be collected. In all three cases, further study may be needed to support management decisions, but this approach appears useful as a general way to identify problems.

Break Points as Evaluative Standards

By plotting perceived crowding against use or encounter levels, it is possible to look for abrupt shifts called "break points," as illustrated in situation A in Figure 4-1 (after Hendee et al. 1978:183). If the percentage feeling crowded remained constant at low use, and then at a certain use or encounter level increased rapidly, that point might be considered a social carrying capacity based on perceived crowding as an evaluative standard. However, such break points may not always exist. If the relationship between use level and perceived crowding is a straight line as illustrated by situation B in Figure 4-1, it would be more difficult to determine capacity on this basis.

Table 4-2. The relationship between use levels and perceived crowding.

Location/Activity	Percent Feeling Moderately or Extremely Crowded Use Level[a]			Correlation Between Use Level and Crowding	Percent of Crowding Explained By Use Levels
	Low	Medium	High		
Grand Canyon[b]	9.5	35.9	32.4	.05	0.3
Rogue River	33.3	21.6	36.9	.20*	4.0
Brule River					
Tubers	0.0	9.3	16.5	.40*	16.0
Canoers	10.4	18.1	33.5	.31*	9.6
Anglers	7.9	34.3	38.6	.41*	16.8
Wisconsin hunters					
Deer	24.6	22.5	27.3	.01	0.0
Goose (firing line)	39.7	71.8	85.3	.44*	19.1
Goose (managed hunt)	3.6	6.1	6.4	.07	0.4

[a]High, medium and low use levels are different across each setting and are described in Chapter 2.
[b]Measured by a single item: "I didn't think we met too many people while on the river."
*p < .05.

Use Levels and Perceived Crowding

The relationships between use levels and perceived crowding provide a basis for assessing the adequacy of the break point approach. The percentages in Table 4-2 show some possibilities. In Grand Canyon, for example, almost 10 percent feel crowded at low use. As use level increases above four hundred per week (to the "medium" category), the number of those feeling crowded more than triples and this remains at about the same level for high use. With only these data, one would be inclined to set social capacity at four hundred or fewer per week, in spite of the low linear relationship. In contrast, Rogue River floaters feel more crowded at low use than people in Grand Canyon do at high use, and there are no break points in the Rogue data, suggesting that capacity has either been exceeded or has not been reached. Given the similarity of the river experience to Grand Canyon, we suspect it has been exceeded.

Perceived crowding for Brule tubers goes up in roughly linear fashion, and the perceived crowding of canoers shows a similar linear trend. Neither case, then, allows identification of a break point capacity. Crowding data for Brule River anglers show a clear break point, increasing more than four times between the low and medium use categories. Based on this criterion, capacity appears to be low use (75 people per day).

Deer hunting shows neither a break point nor a linear trend. Perceived crowding is low for the managed hunt, and it remains low at all use levels observed. Perceived crowding is high on the firing line. Even at low use levels, 40 percent feel moderately or extremely crowded, more than for any other activity at any use level. As use increases to the middle category, the level of crowding jumps to 72 percent, and it stays at this level for high use. This would suggest that the upper bound of the low use category is capacity for a firing line experience. When we compare the figures for the firing line to those for the managed hunt, it appears that the firing line always exceeds capacity for optimal goose hunting.

In summary, percentage data on use levels and crowding for the eight data sets show that the break point method could be used to establish capacity for three activities. For the other five activities, no capacity could be determined using this method.

Encounters and Perceived Crowding

The relationship between encounters and perceived crowding provides additional information which might be useful for setting capacity using crowding as a criterion. As Table 4-3 shows, for all activities except rafting in Grand Canyon, people feel more crowded as contacts increase. These correlations are generally higher than those between use levels and perceived crowding, and in all cases except the firing line reported contact explains at least twice as much variation in crowding as does use level. This makes sense because the number of people one actually sees should have a

Table 4-3. Relationships between contacts and perceived crowding.

| Location/Activity | Percent Feeling Moderately or Extremely Crowded Encounter Level | | | Correlation Between Contacts and Crowding | Percent of Crowding Explained By Contacts |
	Low	Medium	High		
Grand Canyon[a]	.24.7[b]	33.1	34.0	.05	0.03
Rogue River[a]	32.6	15.5	34.9	.12[*]	1.5
Rogue River[r]	16.7	33.0	35.1	.30[*]	9.0
Brule River[r]					
Canoers	5.9	21.5	49.3	.54[*]	29.2
Tubers	1.8	8.2	26.0	.57[*]	32.5
Fishermen	7.4	25.0	60.0	.57[*]	32.5
Wisconsin hunters[r]					
Deer	17.0	22.0	46.5	.46[*]	21.5
Goose (firing line)	47.2	81.3	84.0	.48[*]	22.6
Goose (managed hunt)	3.2	4.1	14.9	.18[*]	3.2

[a]Actual measure by observer.
[b]Measured by a single item: "I didn't think we met too many people while on the river."
[*]$p < .05$.
[r]Reported contacts.

greater impact than the overall number using the area. In most areas managers can change the probability of encounters by manipulating use levels (see Chapter 2), so it appears possible to specify capacity if there are break points for crowding at certain encounter levels.

Several of the activities listed in Table 4-3 show break points where perceived crowding increases disproportionately. For deer hunting, the number feeling moderately or extremely crowded doubles as reported contacts go from medium to high. There are also break points between medium and high contact for the managed hunt and between low and medium contact for the firing line. There are no break points for contacts on the Brule, where the percent feeling crowded increases substantially for each change in contact level. There also appear to be no break points on the Colorado or the Rogue when actual encounters are used as the independent variable. Break points could be used to determine capacities in terms of number of contacts for three of the eight activities.

What Else Makes People Feel Crowded?

Results from our studies show that higher use levels do not always make people feel more crowded. There is a stronger relationship between contacts and perceived crowding, but there are no obvious break points in some cases. Crowding means "too many people," but use levels and contacts do not entirely explain feelings of crowdedness. Why?

Crowding is a complex psychological phenomenon, and it appears that many factors have an effect. In a review of the crowding literature in social psychology, Stockdale (1978) points out that "people can feel crowded in both high and low density environments if the stimulus conditions created by these environments are appropriate for the personal and sociocultural context." This is a technical way of saying that perceived crowding is affected by the personal standards people bring with them and the way they define the setting in question. People can feel crowded even in low-density environments like Grand Canyon because personal and social standards define this as a place where one should see few other people.

Neither use levels nor contacts influence perceived crowding in Grand Canyon. What, if anything, does? To answer this Shelby (1976, 1980) developed a nine-item crowding scale and then selected a set of independent variables correlated with perceived crowding. What personal factors separated those who felt crowded from those who did not?

Table 4-4. Effect of density, interaction and other factors on perceived crowding among Grand Canyon visitors.

	Correlation with Perceived Crowding	Cumulative R^2
Density and Interaction		
People per week leaving Lee's Ferry	.05	
River contacts per day	.05	
People per day seen on river	.05	
Time in sight of people on river	.03	
Percent of all attraction sites with contact	.12*	
Average number of people seen at attraction sites	.13*	
Multiple correlation	.21*	0.04
Preferences and Expectations		
Preferred number of encounters (0-20)	−.50*	
Specific expectation of encounters (0-20)	.30*	
General expectation of encounters (more, same, less than met)	−.47*	0.29
Evaluation of Canyon		
Use impact on environment perceived as high	.64*	
Canyon is not a "wilderness"	.26*	
Multiple correlation	.65*	0.53

*$p < .01$.

Results are shown in Table 4-4. Use levels and river encounters had no significant effect on perceived crowding, but encounters at the attraction sites had a small effect. These variables explain about 4 percent of the variance in perceived crowding. The next group of variables measured users' expectations and preferences: did they see more people than they expected or more than they preferred? Those who said they saw more than they expected or preferred felt much more crowded. These variables were about six times more important than actual contacts, explaining an additional 25 percent of the variance in perceived crowding. In other words, the personal psychological standards people brought with them were more important than the actual number of groups met on the river.

The effects of expectation and preferences in the other study areas have been explored in detail elsewhere (Shelby et al. 1983). In all cases, regression equations including preferences and expectation variables better predict perceived crowding than encounters alone. The large and consistent effect of expectations has interesting implications for management, suggesting that managers can reduce perceived crowding by making user expectations more realistic. Accurate information about the number of people met on a typical trip would allow potential users to either adjust their expectations or select a setting more to their liking. Both would reduce feelings of crowdedness among users of a particular area.

Another way that visitors affect one another is through impacts on the resource. Wide trails or large amounts of litter are evidence that other people have been in an area, whether or not one actually sees them. These perceptions were also important in explaining why people felt crowded; they explained about 24 percent of the variance, increasing the total from 29 percent to 53 percent.

Other studies support these findings. Schreyer and Nielson (1978) explained 19.6 percent of the variance in perceived crowding among floaters in Westwater Canyon, and reported contacts accounted for only one-quarter of this. Findings from their study of Gray and Desolation Canyons were similar. In Yosemite, Lee (1975) found that the amount of horse manure on the trails had a bigger effect on perceived crowding than actual contacts recorded by an observer, and the amount of litter and the evidence of destructive acts also had an effect. These results suggest that perceived crowding is a complex phenomenon, perhaps more closely tied to the psychology of individuals than to the objective characteristics of an area.

Conclusion

Perceived crowding is more useful as an evaluative criterion than satisfaction, primarily because crowding refers more specifically to numbers of people. The problems with this approach revolve around the other personal, social, and situational factors which affect crowding perceptions and the lack of a clear standard for determining the point at which crowdedness reaches unacceptable levels. Both of these problems reduce specificity. The normative approach outlined in the next chapter, which is more specific still, appears to be most useful for developing evaluative standards.

Notes

1. The terms "crowded" and "overcrowded" appear to be used almost interchangeably in both the technical and popular literature on crowding. If crowding is a negative evaluation of a given density, the term "overcrowding" seems redundant, like "irregardless." Popular usage tends to use "overcrowding" when describing crowded conditions in prisons, cities, auditoriums, and so on. When a situation with high density and large numbers of people (described as a "crowd") exceeds certain standards, it is then called "overcrowded." For example, at normal and expected use levels there is a crowd at a Big 10 football game, but only when aisles are full, doors broken down, etc., do people complain of overcrowding. Considering the low density settings we are describing, the term "crowding" is more appropriate than "overcrowding."

2. There would probably be "too few" both times. There is no word in common usage, analagous to the term crowded, that connotes a negative evaluation of the densities that are too low. How does one describe the density at a cocktail party when one arrives first, or at a doubles tennis game with only three people?

3. The crowding concept has been explored most thoroughly in the social psychological literature (see Lawrence 1974, Altman 1975, Stockdale 1978 for reviews). The thrust of these studies has been to determine the effect of independent variables such as density, room size, or interaction pattern on outcome measures such as task performance, effect, or perceived crowding. Sociologists have also looked at the effect of density on a number of outcome variables (Winsborough 1965, Galle et al. 1972). Because the orientation of both psychological and sociological studies is primarily theoretical rather than applied, there has been no attempt to estimate optimal densities for particular settings and, as a result, there are no evaluative standards for deciding how much crowding is too much. Because of this the crowding literature, while useful for understanding the crowding phenomenon, is not very helpful for exploring the capacity issue. We will refer to this literature only when it is directly relevant.

4. This measure was developed for the Brule River study, after the Grand Canyon project was completed. Because of its simplicity and clarity, it has been used in subsequent studies. In Grand Canyon a multiple item scale was used, where responses were combined to create an overall crowding index. This produces a measure which is more reliable statistically, but it makes comparisons among studies more difficult and has less intuitive meaning for policy makers. A single item from the Grand Canyon scale was used to make rough comparisons.

5—Evaluating Use: Contact Preference Standards

Chapter Overview

This chapter describes an approach for evaluating recreation use which focuses more directly on impacts in terms of encounters with other parties. Recreation experiences are viewed as activities regulated and evaluated by social norms. Sometimes these norms are formal, as when the rules of a game specify the number of players, but in most recreation settings they are implicit and need to be determined through research. A number of researchers have developed such standards by asking recreationists about their reactions to different numbers of encounters.

The chapter develops an integrated procedure to specify the social norms used to evaluate encounters. These evaluative standards, which we call encounter preference curves, show both optimal and maximum acceptable levels of contact. They also show the agreement about and intensity of these evaluations. When managers know the level of contact visitors prefer, use levels can be adjusted accordingly, and this becomes the social carrying capacity. When use level is unrelated to contacts, it may be possible to manipulate other management parameters to achieve desired contact levels.

An abbreviated measure of the contact preference curve was used to establish acceptable contact levels for the Colorado and Rogue rivers. In both cases a social carrying capacity was identified. The Colorado River was slightly over capacity, and managers developed a plan to lower daily use and distribute seasonal use so that contacts would not exceed the number identified by the evaluative standard. The Rogue River was substantially above social carrying capacity, but political considerations prevented managers from trying to decrease use. On the Brule River, canoeing use exceeded social carrying capacity on most days, while fishing use was below capacity. For Wisconsin deer hunting, hunters did not agree about the appropriate number of encounters, so Rule 3 (from Chapter 1) was violated. Aside from this, data presented in Chapter 2 showed no relationship between use level and contacts, so social capacity could not be determined even with a clear standard for encounters.

Preference curves can be developed for different types of contacts (e.g. contacts with canoers, horse parties, or motorized rafts). It is also possible to develop separate curves for contacts in different places (such as campsites, attraction sites, or trail heads). In some cases, *these may be more useful for establishing capacities than broader norms for trail, river, or field contacts.*

Contact preference curves are more helpful for establishing social carrying capacities than either satisfaction or perceived crowding. The latter are too general, and they confound evaluation and impact. The contact preference approach is specific, applies to a variety of situations, and avoids some of the conceptual and empirical problems of the other approaches. Capacities can be based on contact preference standards when visitors agree about the type of experience to be provided and the appropriate number of contacts for that experience. If visitors do not agree, conflicts must be resolved before capacities can be established.

Contact Preference Standards

Recreation experiences involve a combination of setting characteristics, social behavior, and individual consciousness. Shared evaluative guidelines, called social norms, help define what is appropriate for different kinds of experiences. The number and distribution of other people is an important and pervasive aspect of recreation experiences which is particularly amenable to a normative approach. Other aspects are also important, and some may be profitably explored using an approach similar to the one developed here. For example, Shelby and Harris (1985, 1986) have applied this model in developing evaluative standards for ecological impacts at wilderness campsites.

A contact preference standard is a normative construct based on shared beliefs about the appropriate number and type of encounters for a particular setting. It is a social norm which characterizes a group and is derived from individual or personal norms. Using techniques described later in this chapter, contact preference standards can be determined for a variety of groups, without those groups or the researchers actually being at the study site. The standard establishes an acceptable level for the number of encounters, and capacity can be specified if use level or some other management parameter affects encounters.

Consider again the idea that different numbers of people create different experiences. What is the right number for a "tennis experience?" It is two if the desired experience is a game of singles. Adding two more changes the game to doubles, a related but somewhat different experience. But what if we increase the number on the court to five? This is no longer tennis as we understand it; the definitions of the game are quite clear with respect to appropriate numbers of people. These numbers are social norms.

Social norms are used to *regulate* behavior (e.g., other players do not go on to tennis courts which already have two or four players) and *evaluate* behavior (if extra players do go on a court someone is likely to notice and complain). Some norms are formalized as rules, while others are informal and might be referred to as "etiquette." Not all recreation experiences are as clearly defined as tennis, but that does not mean norms are absent.

Suppose you are planning a party at your home. If the experience desired is a quiet evening with a close friend or lover, the appropriate number is obviously two. More people (four to twelve) should be invited if the event is a dinner party. A "keg party," however, will probably mean much larger numbers. Different experiences are defined partly in terms of different numbers of people, even in the same setting.

Different numbers of people are also associated with different recreation experiences in natural resource settings. Hiking on backcountry trails in Grand Canyon, it is possible to go for days without seeing anyone, and most would probably agree that this is a kind of wilderness experience. Seeing another party once every day probably would not change this. But what about encountering a steady stream of hikers, camping in large aggregations in designated backcountry camp areas, and waiting in line to use an outhouse in the morning? The right number of encounters for a wilderness experience has been exceeded, and this clearly does not fit the traditional idea of wilderness backpacking.

Contact preference standards formally identify what is informally present in the minds of visitors and managers. In many settings visitors have some idea of the number of people or contacts consistent with a particular kind of experience. For tennis these standards are so well worked out that overtly specifying a social carrying capacity is trivial: everyone understands and abides by the norms. For river running, hunting, and other activities, however, the standards need to be established through research. As Rule 3 indicates, social capacity requires some consensus about appropriate numbers of encounters. To return to our Grand Canyon hiking example, it seems certain that one or two contacts fit with a wilderness experience. But at what point does contact become excessive, and what do we call the experience when it is no longer wilderness? Reasonable consensus often exists, and there are ways to explore this empirically.

Contact preference standards refer to specific experiences. Suppose half the people in a particular setting want a tennis experience and the other half want a volleyball experience. No capacity can be established because there is no agreement about the overall definition of the activity (as Rule 2 indicates). Similarly, capacities for backcountry settings require some agreement about the kind of experience to be provided (often referred to as agreement about management objectives). If some people want a wilderness backpacking experience and others want a developed camping experience, this conflict must be resolved before capacities can be established. It is important to name and define recreation experiences in order to develop evaluative standards for them.

Previous Efforts to Develop Contact Standards

The idea that some kind of standard is needed to determine appropriate encounter levels is not new, and researchers have tried several different ways to develop such criteria. The simplest approach is represented by Lucas's (1964) work in the Boundary Waters Canoe Area (BWCA). He asked people how many encounters they could have and still consider themselves in a wilderness area. "Meeting one party per day was acceptable to 83 percent of the canoeists, and 77 percent could take two groups per day . . . most canoeists said they could not meet any motorboaters without loss of the wilderness atmosphere" (Lucas 1964: 22). With this information, one might set evaluative standards at two contacts with canoes and zero with motorboats. Lucas graphed wilderness ratings at different use levels and concluded that "almost all the canoeists felt themselves in the wilderness if use was something around three hundred groups for three months." His intuitive assessment was that "in an area . . . used by three hundred groups during the summer season, the expected frequency of encounter would probably be between one and two parties per day."

A somewhat more elaborate approach is represented by Stankey's (1973) work. He asked users how they would react to one encounter, two, and so on up to nine encounters. By plotting the percentage indicating a "pleasant" or "very pleasant" experience at each encounter level, he obtained "satisfaction curves." These are essentially contact preference curves showing collective evaluations of different hypothetical encounter levels; Stankey simply chooses "pleasantness" as a general evaluative criterion rather than asking more specifically what amount was preferred or tolerable. A standard can be derived by developing a decision rule such as, "Allowable contact level has been exceeded when less than 50 percent of the users respond favorably."

Stankey's general finding was that users prefer to see few other parties, but most continue to respond positively up to about three encounters per day. In the BWCA, canoeists reacted favorably to three or fewer encounters with paddlers but negatively to any encounters with motorboats. In the Bob Marshall, Bridger, and High Uintas Wilderness areas, most users responded positively to zero to two encounters with backpackers and zero to one encounters with horseback riders. Stankey (1979) used a similar strategy in studies of the Desolation and Spanish Peaks Wilderness areas. Most users would tolerate three contacts per day with hikers in Desolation but only one per day in Spanish Peaks. Tolerances were lower for contacts with horseback parties, and users in both areas agreed that more than one per day was generally unpleasant (this decreased to one every three days for large horse parties). In terms of encounters at camps, 70-80 percent of users in all study areas agreed that "it is most enjoyable not to be camped near anyone else"; most preferred to camp where they could not see or hear other groups.

An approach similar to the one developed in this chapter is represented by the work of Schreyer and Nielson (1978). They asked floaters in Westwater Canyon on the Colorado River and Desolation and Gray Canyons on the Green River, "What do you feel would be an acceptable number of groups to see on the total trip?" This appears to measure tolerable levels rather than preferred or ideal. In Westwater Canyon, 55 percent said three or fewer, while 54 percent of Green River floaters said two or fewer.

Lime and his associates (personal communication) have asked people how satisfied they were with a particular number of contacts in a recreation setting. This is much more specific than (and should not be confused with) overall satisfaction as discussed in Chapter 3. It is a specific contact preference standard, much like the one developed by Stankey. Lime reports that BWCA visitors were less satisfied with higher levels of contacts.

A number of researchers, then, have worked on ways to develop contact standards for backcountry recreation experiences. The approaches vary, but the results consistently show a concern for the issue and general agreement that the appropriate number of encounters is low. The remainder of this chapter develops more explicit evaluative criteria in the form of contact preference standards and shows how they can be used to establish social carrying capacities in the areas we have studied.

Curves to Describe Encounter Norms

In 1965, a social psychologist named Jay Jackson developd a method to describe and quantify the evaluative dimension of social norms. The technique resulted in graphic descriptors of norms which Jackson called return potential curves. We will use this somewhat unwieldy term to refer to Jackson's work, but when using this technique to describe norms related to carrying capacity we will simply refer to encounter or contact preference curves.

An encounter preference curve describing an encounter norm is based on answers to questions which ask people how they feel (favorable or unfavorable) about different numbers of contacts in a specific setting. The curve is generated by plotting the average responses on a graph where the horizontal axis represents number of contacts and the vertical axis shows favorableness of the evaluation. The horizontal axis, then, is the experience dimension, and the vertical axis is the evaluative dimension.

Consider some examples. Figure 5-1 shows hypothetical encounter preference curves for wilderness hiking, a cocktail party in a small room, and walking on a city sidewalk.[1] They can be used to illustrate four important characteristics of encounter norms. The *optimum contact level* is the highest point on the curve, and it represents the ideal situation. The optimum for wilderness hiking is zero contacts and for the small cocktail party it is about twelve. Curves for both activities have relatively sharp peaks, so a single optimal level can be identified. Walking on a city sidewalk is different; here there is no clear optimum.

For activities such as making a call in a phone booth there may be just one level of contact which is acceptable, but for most experiences we would expect people to tolerate some variation. The *range of tolerable contacts* is

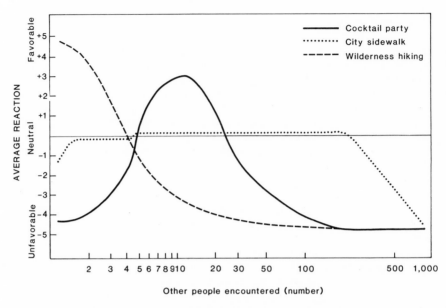

Figure 5-1. Hypothetical encounter preference curves for three activities.

represented by the portion of the curve above the neutral point. For the wilderness hiking experience in our example the range is zero to five contacts, for the cocktail party it is five to twenty-five, and for the sidewalk it is fifty-four to two hundred and fifty. The range of tolerable contacts is useful for establishing capacity because it shows the point at which the average evaluation becomes negative. While a manager might try to provide the optimum level of contact, the point at which contacts exceed the tolerable seems to be an upper limit for evaluative standards. In our hypothetical examples this means five encounters for the wilderness experience, twenty-five for the cocktail party and two hundred and fifty for the city sidewalk.

Contact preference curves also show the degree to which reactions are favorable or unfavorable. The *intensity* of a norm is indicated by the distance of the curve above and below the neutral line. The hypothetical curves show three different intensities. The norm for wilderness hiking is most intense because reactions to encounters range from extremely favorable to extremely unfavorable; we would expect wilderness visitors to be more adamant about the number of contacts because solitude is an important part of wilderness. People at a cocktail party are somewhat less sensitive to encounters, and here intensity ranges from about +3.5 to -5. Norms for encounters on a city sidewalk show low intensity; reactions are generally neutral until there are so many people that it is impossible to travel. Intensity is interesting from a management point of view because it reflects the degree of concern about encounters; the need for control is greater where intensity is high.

Crystallization refers to the amount of agreement about the evaluation of encounters. If all wilderness visitors say that having zero contact is very favorable, then we have maximum agreement at this point. If there were similar agreement at all points on the scale, then the standard is highly crystallized. Crystallization refers to the dispersion of individual evaluations above and below the curve which is plotted through the means. Earlier in the book we pointed out the need for some degree of consensus about evaluation parameters, and crystallization refers to this notion.

Encounter Norms for Brule River Canoers

The Brule River study was the first attempt to use Jackson's return potential model to describe encounter preference curves,[2] so these data best illustrate the various dimensions of the curves. Slightly different data will be used to develop norms for the Colorado and Rogue Rivers.

On the Brule River survey, canoers were asked their reaction to seeing one, two, three, five, seven, nine, fifteen, twenty, and twenty-five other canoers, tubers, or anglers. There were five response categories: very pleasant, pleasant, neutral, unpleasant, and very unpleasant. The measurement technique, unfortunately, is unwieldy; using three groups and nine encounter levels required twenty-seven separate items, identical except for the number and type of encounters.[3] Respondents were quite helpful; only 15 percent of the returned questionnaires had to be discarded because people had failed to answer these questions. Stankey (1973) had a 90 percent completion rate with a similar questionnaire.

Evaluations were averaged at each encounter level, and curves were drawn by connecting these means. Because zero encounters always resulted in the highest evaluation, this was the optimum contact level in all cases. The range of tolerable contact was from zero to the first point where mean evaluation was below neutral. Intensity can be understood intuitively by visually inspecting the distance of a curve above and below the neutral line; this was calculated mathematically by averaging the absolute distances from neutral across the ten contact levels. For crystallization, standard deviations were calculated for the evaluations of each contact level; the standard deviations were then averaged across the ten contact levels.

Curves describing canoer norms for contacts with anglers, tubers, and other canoers are presented in Figure 5-2, and supporting statistics are presented in Table 5-1. The curves all have similar shapes. Zero is the

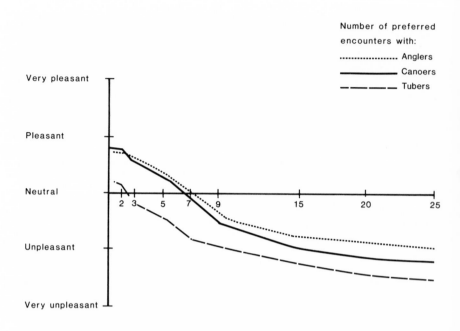

Figure 5-2. Canoers' encounter preference curves.

Table 5-1. Structural properties of Brule River canoers' norms.

| Canoer Evaluations of | Structural Properties of Social Norms | | |
	Tolerable Contacts[a]	Norm Intensity[b]	Norm Crystallization[c]
Fishermen	9	8.0	4.7
Canoers	7	8.9	4.4
Tubers	3	9.9	5.2

[a]Cell frequencies are the number of encounters with the three visitor types that canoers can tolerate.
[b]Cell frequencies are the average intensity levels of the canoers' social norm curves. All three means differ significantly at the $p < 05$ level.
[c]Cell frequencies are the standard deviations around the intensity indices.

optimum contact level, and higher levels are rated as relatively less pleasant. The range of tolerable contact is smallest for encounters with tubers (zero to three); it increases to zero to seven for contacts with other canoers, and zero to nine for contacts with anglers.

Contact norms were held with different intensities. Encounters with tubers provoked the most extreme reactions, resulting in the highest intensity. Encounters with anglers provoked reactions nearer to the neutral line, so intensity here was the lowest. Crystallization for all three encounter norms was fairly comparable, although there was the most consensus about encounters with canoes and the least about those with tubers.

How could these figures be used to establish capacity? *Social capacity would be the level of use producing encounter levels within the tolerable range.* The upper limit of this range is three for contacts with tubers, seven for contacts with canoers, and nine for contacts with anglers. Data on encounter reports were used to see how often these evaluative standards were exceeded. Canoers reported seeing more than three tubers 37 percent of the time, more than seven canoes 76 percent of the time, and more than nine anglers only 5 percent of the time. On the Brule River, it appears that social capacity for canoes is exceeded most of the time and for tubers it is exceeded some of the time. Fishing use appears to be at or below capacity.

Contact Standards for Floaters in Grand Canyon

Two different procedures were used to develop evaluative standards for contacts in Grand Canyon. The first was a single item included in the questionnaire given to floaters before they left the river. It asked how many other parties they preferred to see each day on the river. This preference is roughly analogous to the optimum contact level because it represents an ideal. Responses showed that 34 percent preferred to see no other parties, 15 percent preferred one, 16 percent two, and 13 percent three. In other words, the contact level preferred by the greatest number of users was zero, about two-thirds preferred three or fewer encounters, and more than three-fourths (78 percent) preferred four or fewer.

In the absence of more complete information about user norms, managers decided on three river encounters as the evaluative standard to be used in establishing capacity. This was translated into a use level by consulting the table showing the relationship between use level and contacts reproduced in Chapter 2 (Table 2-4). An average of three river contacts per day results from the medium use level of 401-700 people per week, which translates into approximately 24 trips per week or 3.5 trips per day. To be on the conservative side, managers chose three trips per day as the use limit. Previous limits had allowed seven to eight trips to launch on the busiest days, so this new limit meant a substantial reduction at some times. The proposal was not seriously challenged by the public because the length of the use season was simultaneously extended, allowing overall use (in terms of user days per year) to more than double. Because of these and other changes in river use, a monitoring program was proposed to insure that the plan was meeting the objective of three contacts per day.

The major problem with the preference item as an evaluative criterion was that it did not provide as much detail as the contact preference curves described earlier. The Park Service conducted a series of meetings to assess public reaction to the proposed management plan, providing an opportunity to follow up on the original study and learn more about contact norms. Meetings were held in Flagstaff, Phoenix, Denver, San Francisco, Los Angeles, Salt Lake City, and Washington, D.C. Participation was not limited to users, so there was the potential for including people who had been crowded or displaced off the river.[4]

The questionnaire handed out at the meetings used a modified version of the approach developed in the Brule River study. It told respondents that we were interested in their feelings about encounters with other groups and asked them to indicate the highest number of encounters they would tolerate before their experience changed. Users responded by completing a sentence such as "OK to have as many as _____ river encounters per day."

Analysis of each item produced estimates of the normative characteristics discussed earlier. The optimum contact level was defined as the mode, the category receiving the greatest number of responses. The range of tolerable contacts was from zero to the median response, and crystallization was represented by the standard deviation for each distribution. Norm intensity is not measured by this approach. Because this technique required only one item for each encounter norm, it was possible to learn about encounters occurring in different locations. Five items asked about encounters on the river during the day, time spent in sight of others, the number of stops at which another group might be seen, the chances of meeting others at the most popular stops, and the number of nights spent camping within sight of another party.

Because the "right" number of encounters depends on people's ideas about the kind of experience to be provided, respondents were asked to think of Grand Canyon in different ways. The idea was to specify alternatives to represent three different low-density recreation experiences. It was important to make the alternatives different enough to be realistic possibilities, but also to leave them general enough that people could help define the experience in terms of appropriate encounter levels.

The questionnaire, then, asked people to "imagine the Canyon as a 'wilderness,' a place generally unaffected by the presence of man. If the canyon were this kind of area, which of the following encounter levels would be appropriate? Indicate the *highest* level you would tolerate before the trip would no longer be a *wilderness experience*." After answering the five encounter questions, respondents were asked to "imagine the Grand Canyon as a 'semiwilderness,' the kind of place where complete solitude is not expected.

Table 5-2. Definitions of river experiences in the Grand Canyon.[a]

Question	Wilderness	Semi-wilderness	Undeveloped Recreation
What are appropriate encounter levels in terms of the following:			
River encounters (groups per day)	0.9	2.4	4.0
Hours in sight of others while on river each day	0.5	0.7	1.5
Number of stops (out of 10) with encounters	0.7	2.0	3.8
Chances of meeting 10-30 people at popular places on the river	9%	23%	41%
Number of nights (out of 10) camped near others	0	1.3	3.0

[a]Figures are medians, which can be read as "50 percent would tolerate _____ or fewer" encounters, hours in sight, etc.

In this case, which encounter levels would be appropriate? Indicate the *highest* level you would tolerate before the trip would no longer be a *semiwilderness experience.*" Finally, respondents were asked to "imagine the Grand Canyon as an 'undeveloped recreation area,' the kind of place where a natural setting is provided but meeting other people is part of the experience . . . . Indicate the point at which there would be too many people for even this kind of *undeveloped recreation experience.*" With a short questionnaire (just fifteen items), it was possible to obtain information about three different alternatives, each defined by five kinds of encounters. Subjects were then asked to indicate which experience they felt was currently available and which they thought should be provided.

Responses defining the three experiences are summarized in Table 5-2. These figures are medians, which can be read as "50 percent would tolerate _____ or fewer" encounters, hours in sight, etc. For example, respondents defined wilderness as one or fewer river encounters per day, less than one-half hour in sight of others on the river, meeting other parties at no more than one out of ten attraction sites, a 10 percent chance of meeting others at the most popular stops, and camping away from other parties virtually all of the time. Appropriate contact levels were higher for semiwilderness and undeveloped recreation.

The cumulative frequency distributions presented in Table 5-3 provide still another view, and here we can see the options for establishing an evaluative standard. Line "a" shows the majority standard; 50 percent would tolerate one or fewer contacts for a wilderness experience, three or fewer for semiwilderness, and four or fewer for undeveloped recreation.

Table 5-3. Cumulative frequencies for tolerable river contacts in Grand Canyon.

Maximum Preferred Contacts		Type of Experience		
		Wilderness	Semiwilderness	Undeveloped Recreation
0		23.8	1.9	2.2
1	a	53.9	14.0	8.3
2		78.3	40.5	18.1
3		88.4	64.5	36.8
4	b	92.5	79.8	49.5
5		95.1	90.3	70.8
6-10		98.8	97.5	93.3
11		100.0	100.0	100.0

[a]Higher contact levels exceed standards for a majority.
[b]Higher contact levels exceed standards for 90 percent.

This is the upper end of the tolerable range, the level which managers should aim for. Line ''b'' describes another criterion which is probably excessively high. For 90 percent of respondents, more than four contacts exceeds the wilderness standard, more than five contacts exceeds the semiwilderness standard, and more than ten exceeds the standard for even an undeveloped recreation experience. If managers want to provide an opportunity for a wilderness experience, then, they should aim for one contact per day and avoid exceeding four. For a semiwilderness experience they should aim for three contacts per day and not exceed five; and for undeveloped recreation they should aim for four and not exceed ten.

The Grand Canyon example, then, satisfies Rule 1 with data showing the relationship between use and encounters. It also satisfies Rule 3 with evaluative standards for three different kinds of experiences. The remaining issue is Rule 2; is there agreement about the type of experience to be provided?

The vast majority of river users (91 percent) consider the canyon a wilderness, and they generally see it as a setting where developments and conveniences are out of place. Only 10 percent felt there should be more developments like Phantom Ranch, and only 7 percent favored building a tram into the canyon. A similarly small number favored more conveniences (9 percent) and better facilities (12 percent) on river trips. There was similar agreement among meeting participants who filled out the questionnaires. Asked which type of recreation experience managers *should* provide, 60 percent said wilderness, 34 percent said semiwilderness, and 6 percent said undeveloped recreation.

Meeting participants were also asked what type of experience is *currently* provided. Fifty-four percent said semiwilderness, and 26 percent said undeveloped recreation, and 20 percent said wilderness. Most floaters run the river during the high-use periods, averaging about five river contacts per day; this is close to the number defining the semiwilderness and undeveloped recreation experiences. The experience labels that people apply to the current experience, then, fit with the actual encounter levels they were likely to have had.

It is one thing to want a wilderness experience, but when this means limiting numbers people will have to give something up. Individuals who attended the meetings were asked, "If you prefer wilderness, would you be willing to do any of the following things in order to accomplish this?" Sixty-eight percent said they would wait a year longer to go on the trip, 56 percent said they would pay $100 more for the trip, and 55 percent said they would go during the winter season (October-May). When faced with the prospect of doing one of these things or having a semiwilderness experience, 57 percent said they would rather wait, pay more, or go during the winter; this is a strong statement about the kind of experience preferred. From all of this it seems safe to conclude that people agree that river trips in Grand Canyon should provide a wilderness experience.

The evaluative standard based on normative data from the public meetings is similar to the standard discussed earlier which was based on the single contact preference item contained in the questionnaire administered on site. The preference-based standard suggested that managers should try to keep encounters at three or less per day, and the norm-based standard suggested that they should aim for one per day and avoid exceeding four. The advantage of the more elaborate normative approach is that it gives more detail and supplies information about alternative experiences. The data also support the idea that different contact levels are appropriate for different kinds of experiences, even with the same activity in the same location.

Managers chose a level of three launches per day, which was expected to produce the desired contact level of about three per day. There was some uncertainty about this because launch levels would be more consistent (at three, without high-use days up to seven or eight), so it was important to monitor contact rates to insure that they met evaluative standards.[5]

Contact Preference Standards for the Rogue River

An evaluative standard for the Rogue was developed with the same approach used at Grand Canyon public meetings. River runners were asked to give their highest tolerable contact levels for wilderness, semiwilderness, and undeveloped recreation. Responses defining these three experiences in terms of the five types of contacts are summarized in Table 5-4.

The most striking thing about these figures is their resemblance to those defining Grand Canyon experiences. The Rogue as a resource is considerably different from Grand Canyon, and responses are from a user population rather than from persons attending public meetings. In spite of this, contact

Table 5-4. Definitions of river experiences on the Rogue.[a]

Question	Wilderness	Semi-wilderness	Undeveloped Recreation
What are appropriate encounter levels in terms of the following:			
Encounters per day	1.8	2.7	4.2
Hours in sight of others while on the river	0.3	1.0	1.8
Number of stops (out of 5) with encounters	1.0	2.0	2.7
Chances of meeting 5-20 people at places like Tate Creek	11%	30%	50%
Number of nights (out of 5) camped near others	0.4	1.4	2.6

[a]Figures are medians, rounded for clarity (commercial passengers only).

norms for the three experiences are remarkably similar. Further work is needed to see how well these findings generalize to other settings and other activities (see Shelby 1981a for further discussion).

On the Rogue, the number of contacts most frequently chosen by users (the modal category) is one to two for a wilderness experience, two for semiwilderness, and three or six to ten for undeveloped recreation. The cumulative frequency distributions presented in Table 5-5 show the options for evaluative standards. Using the majority (line "a") and 90 percent (line "b") standards as before, managers trying to provide a wilderness experience should aim for two or fewer encounters and avoid exceeding four. Similarly for a semiwilderness experience they should aim for three and not exceed five, and for undeveloped recreation they should aim for four and not exceed six to ten.

All the findings discussed above are from commercial float trip passengers. The reader will recall, however, that commercial jet boats share the lower 12 miles of the wild section of the river with floaters. We have shown that norms differ for different experiences, even when the activity and the place remain the same. What about a different activity, like jet boating? For a wilderness experience, 50 percent of the floaters would tolerate 1.8 or fewer river encounters per day. In contrast, 50 percent of the jet boaters would tolerate 4.4 contacts. This tolerance seems related to structural differences in the two activities. Jet boats travel further and faster in a day, so they have more encounters; accordingly, jet boaters are willing to tolerate a higher number. The norm held by jet boaters is also less crystallized. Floaters' responses ranged from zero to ten, while those of jet boaters ranged from zero to one hundred; the standard deviation for floaters is 2.0, and for jet boaters it is 24.9. All of our data show less crystallization for higher-contact experiences, suggesting that norms are less specific as the number of encounters goes up.

What kind of experience should be available on the Rogue? Data show less consensus here than there was for Grand Canyon. The majority of *commercial* floaters (57 percent) think the river should provide a wilderness experience, while 41 percent think it should provide a semiwilderness experience. Among *private* floaters, however, only 39 percent favor wilderness, and 52.7 percent favor semiwilderness. When these findings are combined according to the groups' representation in the general user population, 48 percent favor wilderness and 45 percent favor semiwilderness. In addition, Rogue River runners are less willing than Grand Canyon floaters to pay a price to achieve their desired contact levels. Sixty percent said they would wait a month longer to go on the trip, and 55 percent would take the trip in May or September. However, only 40 percent were willing to follow a schedule while on the river and only 28 percent would pay $50 more. The result is a less clear fulfillment of Rule 3, which requires agreement about the kind of experience which should be available. The only clear agreement is that the experience should not be undeveloped recreation.

Taking the evaluative standards for wilderness (aim for two encounters a day and do not exceed four) and semiwilderness (aim for three encounters a day and do not exceed five), is it possible to develop capacity figures for the Rogue? Referring to Table 2-3 in Chapter 2, the lowest use level (one to four trips, or zero to sixty people, per day) results in an average of 7.5 contacts per day. This *exceeds* the standard for both wilderness and semiwilderness. The average contact level on the Rogue was 10.5 per day, which exceeds even the standard for undeveloped recreation. It appears that social carrying capacity has been exceeded on the Rogue, and this explains why people viewed it as one of the most crowded areas we studied (see Table 3-1),

Table 5-5. Cumulative frequencies for tolerable river contacts on the Rogue River.

		Type of Experience	
Maximum Preferred Contacts	Wilderness	Semiwilderness	Undeveloped Recreation
0	16.1	1.4	1.5
1	43.0	17.1	7.4
2 a	70.4	45.7	20.3
3	84.3	64.6	42.1
4 b	88.6	72.4	54.0
5	94.7	87.1	70.3
6-10	100.0	97.7	91.1
10+	100.0	100.0	100.0

[a]Higher contact levels exceed standards for majority.
[b]Higher contact levels exceed standards for 90 percent.

second only to the firing line goose hunt. Table 2-3 does not specify a capacity figure because the lowest category produces contact levels in excess of evaluative standards, but it appears that two to three trips (fifteen to thirty people) per day is about right. Current use limits on the Rogue allow one hundred and twenty people per day, and managers seem to feel that lowering this is not feasible politically. This does not mean that people do not enjoy the Rogue; users report the highest satisfaction level of any area we studied (see Chapter 3 for a discussion of the problems of using satisfaction as an evaluative standard). But it is quite clear that encounter levels exceed norms for desired experiences, and use levels exceed social carrying capacity.

Problems with Capacity for Deer Hunters

The attempt to establish capacity for deer hunters in Wisconsin is hampered by two factors. First, there is no clear evaluative criterion like those found on the Colorado and Rogue Rivers. Hunters were asked about the number of contacts they preferred, but responses showed no consensus; 17 percent preferred to see no other hunters, while another 18 percent preferred to see eleven or more. This lack of agreement makes it difficult to specify the appropriate encounter level.

Even though there is no clear agreement among deer hunters about encounter norms, collecting normative data makes it possible to document an important difference in definitions of hunting experiences. It appears that one group views deer hunting as a rather solitary experience; this group prefers few encounters. Another group believes that the presence of other hunters helps to move deer, thereby increasing the likelihood of seeing game. This group prefers to have a larger number of encounters. The bimodal distribution of encounter preferences documents this difference in norms, and suggests that this conflict in experience definitions would have to be resolved (perhaps by creating separate areas) before capacity could be established.

Data on another social impact are similarly inconclusive. Hunters were asked several questions about the extent to which other hunters "got in the way." These items were combined into an "interference" scale, and responses were compared for different contact levels. At zero to four contacts, 44 percent reported low interference and only 22 percent reported high interference. At five to nine contacts, however, this reverses; now 21 percent report low interference and 50 percent report high interference. This trend continues, and at twenty or more contacts 72 percent report high interference.

Is it possible to establish an evaluative standard on this basis? The logical point is at five or more contacts, where the number reporting high interference first outweighs the number reporting low interference. However, this experience parameter is much like perceived crowding; the term "interference" confuses impact with an implicit negative evaluation, and we really do not know how much interference is too much. The result is that there is no clear evaluative standard for either contacts or interference; hunters do not show the clear agreement about encounter norms which are required to satisfy Rule 3 for setting capacity.

The other major problem with establishing capacity for deer hunting is the lack of relationship between management parameters and impacts in terms of encounters. As discussed in Chapter 2, densities (hunters per square mile in large management units) are not correlated with reported encounter levels. Even if an appropriate number of encounters could be specified, managers are currently unable to produce changes in contact levels by manipulating the numbers of hunters in game management units. Redesigning the units or altering management practices might change this, but for now deer hunting in Wisconsin fails to satisfy Rule 1 as well as Rule 3, and a social capacity cannot be specified. Capacities could perhaps be established for smaller units with hunters showing similar encounter preferences.

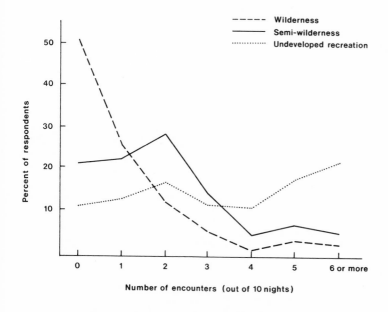

Figure 5-3. Camp encounter norms for Grand Canyon.

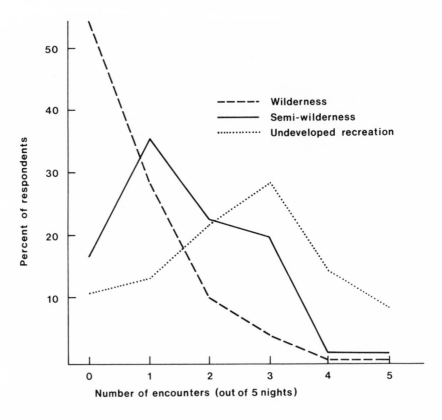

Figure 5-4. Camp encounter norms for the Rogue River.

Capacities Based on Camp Encounters

The capacities discussed so far have been based on evaluative standards for encounters which occur while traveling during the day. However, norms for these kinds of encounters are not always highly crystallized; users do not always agree about the appropriate number of trail or river contacts. Stankey (1973) shows that encounters at camps are evaluated more negatively than contacts on trails. Lucas (personal communication) points out that camps are essentially temporary "residences." People are willing to share streets, sidewalks, and other public areas, but they want greater privacy in their yards and more still inside their houses. Camp encounters may therefore be important social impacts.

Camp contact preferences for the Colorado and Rogue rivers are shown in Figures 5-3 and 5-4. The tolerances for the wilderness experience show a great deal of agreement. Over 50 percent of the respondents said the appropriate number of contacts is zero, and any higher number changes the experience. This kind of crystallization makes for a clear and defensible evaluative standard, given that most people agreed Grand Canyon should offer a wilderness experience and that a stated management objective for the Rogue is to allow river parties to camp alone.

Social carrying capacity can be established on this basis, but the approach is somewhat different. The reader will recall that camp contacts on both the Colorado and Rogue were not correlated with use levels. Instead, contacts appear to be a function of the location and geographic characteristics of sites. As a result, capacity can be established only if we know how other management parameters affect camp contact rates.

The most effective management mechanism in this case is scheduling. To schedule effectively one should first designate campsites which are secluded from one another. Given information about distances traveled each day, it is then possible to estimate the number of launches per day which will fill the campsite system. This was done with a computer simulation model in Grand Canyon, although managers decided against this type of capacity because of the severe regimentation involved. On the Rogue, the Bureau of Land Management has for several seasons asked users to list their intended camps. These informal scheduling data could be used to arrive at a capacity estimate, although managers have been reluctant to establish formal campsite scheduling, again because of the regimentation involved.

Notes

1. This diagram and discussion were first presented in a paper given by Heberlein at the River Recreation Management and Research Symposium held in Minneapolis on January 24-27, 1977, and they were published in the proceedings for that meeting (USDA Forest Service General Technical Report NC-28).

2. Brule River data were collected with the assistance of Jerry Vaske (1977), and the discussion of contact preference curves builds on his Masters thesis work done at Wisconsin with Heberlein.

3. We have since developed a procedure for asking only one question which for large samples allows calculation of a contact preference curve. See Appendix 1.

4. Managers counted 1,107 people in attendance at these meetings. Because of restrictions on questionnaires used by federal agencies, individuals could not be required to fill out the questionnaires, nor could repeated contacts be used to increase response rates. The questionnaire was described as "voluntary," for citizens wanting to register their opinions. Unfortunately only 37 percent of those attending returned a completed questionnaire. It should be noted that only 61 percent of those attending filled out name and address cards to register as participants; our sample is 64 percent of this group.

5. Results of the River Management Plan remain speculative since the plan was overturned by Congress prior to its implementation. See Chapter 6 (pages 102-107) for details.

6—Moving Ahead with Carrying Capacity Research

Chapter Overview

Researchers and managers considering carrying capacity studies are faced with three questions not yet addressed in this book: (1) How can the model be applied to other settings and activities? (2) What unresolved research issues should be explored in further work? and (3) What is the best way to see that research is actually used in the policy-making process? This chapter addresses these questions.

To show how the model can be applied, eight diverse activities were selected in five outdoor and three indoor settings. They include a reservoir, ski area, picnic area, hot spring, a wilderness backpacking area, an eating establishment, a swimming pool, and a tavern. For each setting, the model helps identify impact parameters, evaluative standards, and the type of capacity likely to be most limiting. The process for establishing capacities is summarized.

There are a number of unresolved research issues in carrying capacity research. They include replicating and extending the model, encounter norms, other dimensions which define experiences, reported versus actual contacts, the satisfaction concept, expanding the sampling domain beyond current users, the role of individual differences, developing more effective and less expensive research methods, and deciding when capacity studies should be done.

The interaction between research and policy is explored using the Grand Canyon as a case study. Lessons from this experience range from establishing communications between researchers, managers, and the public to the role of research in representing the views of less vocal individuals and groups.

Applying the Model in Other Areas

The model presented in this book is general enough for activities as different as hunting and river running, so it should work for other activities in other settings. Applying the model in more diverse circumstances is the next step in advancing understanding of the carrying capacity issue. For example, Heberlein and his associates (in press) have recently used the model to estimate carrying capacity for recreational boating in the Apostle Island National Lakeshore. This twenty-two-island archipelago in Lake Superior is

Table 6-1. Examples of carrying capacity measures for other areas.

| Area/Activity | Management Parameters | | Impact Parameters | | | | Type of Capacity/ Evaluate Standard |
	Use Level	Other	Ecological	Physical	Facility	Social	
Cove Palisades/ water skiing, camping	Boats launched per day	Speed limits, wakeless boats, skiers must stay directly behind boats	Carbon monoxide from exhaust, litter on beach	Water space per boat, beach space per party	Picnic spaces per group, time waiting for fuel	Disturbance from wakes, space for skiers to turn	Social (one wake every quarter mile of skiing, 100 ft. each side of boat)
Bachelor Butte/ skiing	Lift tickets per day	Reduce parking, operate lifts at different speeds	Wildlife observed, diversity of plant species	Space per person on slopes, in life line areas	Cars per parking space, people per chair or lift	Time in lift lines, encounters during descent	Facility (2 or 3 people per chair), social (20 min. line)
Roslyn Lake/ picnicking, swimming, softball	People per hour entering park	Encourage car pooling, group size limits	Litter, erosion along lake shore	Square feet of grass per person, feet of shore line per person	Cars per parking of water system	People per game person in group picnic areas	Facility (one car per space, water system remains operative)
Austin Hot Springs/ soaking	Persons per hour entering through parking area	Construct "dividers" in pools	Percent of vegetation trampled, water quality in pools	Square feet per person in pools	Cars per parking space, persons per rest room	Groups per pool, confrontations between nude and clothed soakers	Social (one group per pool, but this changes as use increases; no confrontations)
Jefferson Park/ backpacking	Total number in Jefferson Park	No camp fires, no camping in meadows, no camping within 100 ft. of lakes	Bare ground at camps, amount of available firewood	Flat space available for tents	(No facilities provided)	Number of other parties camped within sight	Social (no more than 2 other parties in sight)
Country Store Deli & Restaurant/ eating	Total customers in restaurant	Place tables outside (nice weather only), replace large tables with small ones	Smoke in air, wear on floor	Floor space per person	People per table, time waiting for food	People per food service area, groups per table	Facility (one person per seat, 5-10 minute waiting time)
Aquatic Center/ swimming	Number signed in who haven't signed out	Install bulkhead to separate conflicting activity	Dirt and bacteria in water, filter cleanings per day	Water space per person	People per locker, people per lifeguard	People per team (water polo), evasive action by lap swimmers	Social (6 people per team, no evasive actions)
Squirrel's Tavern/ playing pool	Number in second floor pool-playing area	Move pinball machines downstairs, encourage nonplayers to wait downstairs to be paged	Air quality, garbage on tables and floors	Floor space per person	People per table, people per cue stick, space for those waiting	Jostling around tables, time waiting to play	Facility (2-4 people per table, one person per cue), social (3 quarters on table)

served by five marinas on the Wisconsin coast. Following the basic model and using preference for contacts with other boats at popular mooring sites among the islands as the evaluative criterion, it was determined that an additional two hundred marina slips could be added before social capacity was reached.

To help managers and researchers see how the model might be applied to a diverse range of recreation activities and settings, we spent a summer observing a variety of sites near Corvallis, Oregon.[1] The goal here was not to actually carry out capacity studies, but to investigate a diversity of activities and settings and provide examples of management parameters and the four types of impact parameters in situations dramatically different from those already discussed in this book (see Table 6-1). The final column in the table reflects our judgment about the most limiting type of capacity, which varies from one area to the next. The text is organized by area, but those interested in illustrations of specific elements of the model can simply read down the appropriate column of Table 6-1.

Eight activities were selected, five outdoor—a reservoir, a ski area, a picnic area, hot springs, and a backpacking area—and three indoor—an eating establishment, a swimming pool, and a tavern. For each setting, the model helps identify key variables and limiting factors. The goal here is to go beyond the detailed technical sections of the first five chapters and see how the capacity model can be applied to virtually any recreation setting.

Cove Palisades State Park is on a reservoir in central Oregon. The area is well known for its desert-canyon scenery, but water-skiing is the most popular recreation activity. Use level was defined as the number of boats per day launching from the campground boat ramp. Ecological impacts (such as carbon monoxide from exhausts) are minimal, and one could physically fit hundreds of boats into the area. Limiting impact parameters are the time spent waiting to refuel (facilities) and interference from boat wakes and the space needed for skiers to make turns (social). Carrying capacity would probably be best calculated on the basis of evaluative standards for these social impacts. Skiers want relatively smooth water (although they do not mind crossing wakes occasionally), and they need room for the maneuvers that add challenge to the sport (at least 100 feet on each side of the boat). One could increase the number of boats if skiers followed right behind their own boat, constantly bumping across the wakes of others, but that would not be much of a skiing experience.

Bachelor Butte is the most popular ski area in Oregon. Use level is easily measured as the number of lift tickets sold each day. The most important impacts involve facilities (parking lots and lifts) and social factors (time spent in lift lines). Since the addition of a new parking lot, the limiting factor now appears to be lift capacity. Lifts can handle only two or three people per chair and have a maximum speed, so lines form when there are more skiers than the lift can accommodate. When waiting time exceeds twenty to thirty minutes people begin to grumble and feel cheated. Increasing the top speed of lifts is a management parameter that might help alleviate the problem but the plan is to expand facilities by building more lifts.

Roslyn Lake is a small day-use picnic area owned by Portland General Electric Company. It is particularly popular for large social gatherings such as company picnics and family reunions. Ecological impacts like shoreline erosion are minimal and the amount of physical space available is considerable; and social impacts are probably not the limiting factor because recreation activities are generally unaffected by contact with other people. It appears that capacity is reached when all parking spaces are filled and when use of restrooms overtaxes the water system and leaves toilets inoperative. These parking and restroom capacities are reached long before people consider the area to be beyond social capacity for a large group picnic experience. Angry confrontations occur between visitors and attendants when failed restrooms are locked up or visitors are told that they must park outside and walk. Facility capacity is, of course, one of the easiest to increase, but for financial reasons that is unlikely in this case. Another solution is to encourage carpooling, which would help the parking problem but not the water system.

Austin Hot Springs is a semideveloped day-use area in the Cascade Mountains. Located between a highway and the Clackamas River are eight to ten soaking pools that have been built by stacking river rocks; they change with water levels and user modifications. This is one of the few cases where physical capacity is a limiting factor; a hot spring is clearly full when there is no longer any room to sit and soak. Social impacts are also critical. When there are few users, people limit themselves to one group per pool. But when more people enter the area and all the pools are occupied, the norm (and the experience) changes and groups begin to share pools. Social capacity is reached when there is one group per pool, while physical capacity is reached as people fill all spaces large enough to sit and soak. There is also a larger pool on the other side of the river. It provides a more secluded location and the one group norm is more pervasive here. One way to increase the social capacity of the hot springs would be to build stone dividers in this large pool to create more smaller pools, but that would destroy the secluded single-group experience.

Jefferson Park is a mile-long subalpine meadow in the Mt. Jefferson Wilderness. It is a popular overnight destination for backpackers because of its numerous lakes, spectacular scenery, and close proximity to several trail heads. Use level was defined as the total number in Jefferson Park, although it would also be possible to consider use levels for each of the lakes individually. Ecological impacts include bare ground at camps and the amount of available firewood; these can be minimized by management parameters such as restricting camp locations and requiring users to carry stoves. Physical capacity can be assessed in terms of available flat space for tents, particularly around lakes where most users prefer to camp; it is not a limiting factor since utilizing every square foot of flat space for tents would result in extremely high use. Facility impact is not an issue since no facilities are provided. Social impact can be measured in terms of the number of other parties camped within sight. Surveys of user preferences show that most would choose to have no more than two other parties in sight, so capacity would be the use level which limited camp encounters to this number. The geographical layout of camps and land features which screen the sight and sound of other groups would obviously play an important part in the capacity determination.

The Country Store is a small eating establishment. It contains a bakery, ice cream parlor, delicatessen, and "Mexicatessen," as well as tables and chairs. Customers get their food at one of the four service counters and then find a place to sit and eat. Physical space and ecological impacts (such as smoke in the air) do not appear to be limiting factors here; facility and social impacts are more restrictive. Time spent waiting to be served is an important facility impact because people wait in line at the counters rather than sitting at tables as they would in a full service restaurant. The seating capacity defined by the number of chairs at each table is another limiting factor, but the social capacity of the tables is often lower than the facility capacity. Most people prefer to sit with only those in their own group, even though there may be more chairs at the table. This is particularly true at the large tables, which have four to five chairs but are often occupied by only two or three people. One way to increase capacity would be to replace the large tables with smaller ones which might be more fully utilized.

The Corvallis Aquatics Center is a typical swimming facility. Here ecological impacts such as dirt and bacteria in the water are important. The chlorination and filtering systems are management parameters that keep these biological impacts in line with health department standards without limiting use. People per locker and people per lifeguard are two important facility impact parameters. Locker rooms are more than adequate, so facility capacity is only an issue when lifeguards are short-handed. Social capacity appears to be the limiting factor for specialized activities such as water polo (where two teams of six people occupy the whole pool) and lap swimming (where swimmers do not want to have to stop or take evasive action). For open and family swimming, where the activity is defined in terms of more random splashing around, social capacity increases and physical or facility capacity becomes the limiting factor.

Squirrel's Tavern has a bar and tables on the first floor and a pool room with some other games and additional seating on the second floor. Facilities in the form of adequate tables and cue sticks are the obvious limiting factor for pool room capacity, but observation turned up some interesting social factors. People who want to play when the tables are already full signify this by laying a quarter on the edge of the table. Others follow suit, and at busy times the quarters begin to line up. Prospective players can see how long they will have to wait by the number of quarters on the table, and when there are more than three (indicating a 45-minute or longer wait) people start grumbling and leaving. Jostling around the tables as players try to get in position for shots is another problem which indicates that too many people are waiting. This could be alleviated by encouraging people to wait in the bar downstairs and then paging them, but this solution might not work because people like to watch others play.

Carrying Capacity Assessment Process (C-CAP)

Those interested in setting up capacity studies will need to consider the proposed site in detail. The following process discusses the specific steps for capacity determination suggested by the model presented in this book (those interested in greater detail should consult Appendices 1 and 2). The process has some common elements with other resource planning or assessment processes, including the limits of acceptable change (Stankey and McCool 1984) and visitor impact management (Graefe et al. 1983) schemes.

(1) *Organize and evaluate background information.* This process includes existing information on the geographic context, management structures, political climate, use patterns and trends, and so on. A framework for accomplishing this task is presented in Appendix 2.

(2) *Identify in general terms the type of experience opportunity to be provided.* This includes a review of legal mandates, agency guidelines, and management objectives, as well as the spectrum of recreation opportunities possible within resource capabilities. Establishing capacity requires a single objective or a compatible set of objectives; disagreement about what should be provided constitutes a use conflict which must be resolved first. Data collected later (step 4a) will help to further refine and specify management objectives.

(3) *Identify important impacts*—ecological, physical, facility, or social. Sources for this information may include the public at large, interest groups, managers, agency records and files, etc. The task here is to specify current or anticipated problems or the unique characteristics or values of the resource. This list should be narrowed down to a group of measurable impact parameters for which data will be collected.

(4) *Collect data* in the following categories (specific measurement techniques for carrying capacity variables are discussed in Appendix 1):

a. Type of experience opportunity to be provided, if not clearly specified in step 2. This kind of information is particularly helpful where there is disagreement about management objectives, either between managers and the public or among public interest groups. These data will help document the extent of agreement or disagreement. Results here should be used in conjunction with information from step 2 to refine management objectives and resolve conflicts.

b. Evaluative standards. The normative approach outlined in Chapter 5 can be used to develop standards for a variety of impact problems. Standards should be developed for the critical impacts identified in step 3.

c. Existing conditions. Collect the descriptive data outlined in Chapter 2 to show the range of variation for management parameters and impact parameters as well as the relationships between these variables. This will document the extent of current impacts and suggest the management strategies which might help control them.

(5) *Develop management alternatives* which would limit impacts to acceptable levels. These alternatives should include use limits and other management strategies which would control impacts.

(6) *Select a management strategy.* If the strategy includes a use limit, that

level of use is the carrying capacity. If other management parameters are used to help control impacts, they should be specified as part of the management plan.

(7) *Monitor impacts* to insure that they fall within acceptable limits and adjust management policies if necessary.

Unresolved Research Issues

This book has combined a number of separate data collection efforts into a single model. The goal has been to integrate and simplify, but research is never quite that tidy; there are always unanswered questions.

The most obvious need is to replicate and extend the carrying capacity model in other settings. The examples described earlier in this chapter suggest that this can be done, but more diversity would be better still. We are currently involved in studies of sail boating (Heberlein et al. in press), backpacking (Shelby and Harris 1985, 1986), and more developed river running (Shelby and Stein 1984).

Aside from capacity studies, information is needed about contact norms for other activities. A regional or national study identifying norms for a true cross-section of recreation pursuits would be tremendously helpful, independent of descriptive data. It is also important to study the same activities in different settings to see if norms are stable regardless of location. If they are, capacity studies could be done simply by collecting descriptive data. Studies on the Colorado, Rogue, and Illinois rivers, for example, suggest that norms for certain kinds of river running experiences are similar in these three locations (Shelby 1981a). Is this true for other activities?

More research is needed on the impacts of different types of contact. For the studies in this book we have generally made the simplifying assumption that all contacts have the same impact, but in practice this is rarely the case. Data from the Brule River study show that norms differ for encounters with canoers, tubers, and anglers. Other studies suggest different impacts for parties on horseback and those on foot, large or small parties, and those using motorized or nonmotorized vehicles. Graefe et. al. (1984a) cite over thirty studies which show that some kinds of encounters have a greater impact than others. This is most likely to happen when the two groups are engaged in different activities in the same setting, such as paddling canoeists and motorboaters, anglers and canoers, backpackers and parties on horseback, or skiers and snowmobilers. Social differences such as norms, group size, experience levels, status levels, and values can also play a role. Theoretical work is needed to discover the social and psychological reasons for the disproportionate effect of different types of encounters.

Work on encounters should also be expanded to include the timing and location of contacts. Chapter 5 shows different norms for river and camp contacts, and backcountry studies (Stankey 1973) show different norms for trail and camp contacts. Shelby and Harris (1986) show different norms for ecological impacts at different locations within the same wilderness area. Reasons for these differences should be a focus of further study.

There may also be important differences for experiences within activity types. In the Colorado and Rogue rivers studies we found that norms varied depending on whether the experience was defined as wilderness, semi-wilderness, or undeveloped recreation. There are certainly analogous differences for other activities which need to be specified and defined empirically.

There are other dimensions besides encounter levels which define experiences. Clark and Stankey (1979) explore factors such as levels of development, rules and regimentation, other resource uses, and so on. Ideally, normative definitions of all these factors would describe the conditions managers need to provide. Considerable conceptual and empirical work remains to be done here.

Another issue involves the reported versus actual contact measures described in Chapter 2. At higher use levels visitors report only about half the contacts recorded by a trained observer. These findings raise theoretical questions and present practical problems for establishing social carrying capacity. On the theoretical side, more research is needed to account for the discrepancy between observers and visitors. Some contacts may be more psychologically relevant than others. More research is needed to further document this discrepancy and test alternative theories which might account for the difference.

The difference between reported and actual contacts also raises an important practical problem. If contacts are used as the impact parameter, which measure should managers use to establish carrying capacity? Should carrying capacity be based on what is actually happening or what visitors think is happening? Why are these two measures different? Are there ways to improve the accuracy of self-reports? Do visitors always underreport as severely as they did on the Rogue River? Is there some constant that can be added to visitor self-reports? Do people feel more crowded when a capacity is set based on perceived rather than actual contact levels?

The concept of satisfaction with recreation experiences also needs further attention. For example, as visitors left the Brule River, we asked them how satisfied they were with their trip. Five months later, using a mailed questionnaire, we again asked exactly the same question. This is essentially a test, retest reliability check: the same measure used at two points in time. With intelligence quotients or other cognitive measures one expects test, retest correlations in the range of .60 - .80. For the Brule sample, however, the correlation was .29. This suggests that either (1) satisfaction, as operationalized with a single global measure, is an unreliable construct; or (2) satisfaction when people leave a recreation setting is different from satisfaction after they have had a chance to reflect on the experience. If satisfaction is unreliable, it is not a very useful scientific construct. If, on the other hand, there are two different kinds of satisfaction with recreation experiences, that might be an interesting issue to pursue.

In response to the Brule findings, in the Rogue River study we included the satisfaction item in the on-site interview and in two different places on the follow-up questionnaire. Correlations between the on-site measure and the two follow-up measures were .38 and .37, which is comparable to the Brule finding. The correlation between the two follow-up measures, however, was .87. This suggests the measure is reliable, but that the concept is either unstable or changes meaning over time.

Stankey and McCool (1984) note that both the conceptualization and measurement of satisfaction are problematic in the carrying capacity literature. A single item indicator may have skewed distributions, which limits the ability of any independent variable to influence satisfaction level. They further argue that satisfaction is a multidimensional construct which cannot be measured well with a single item indicator. Finally they note that dissatisfaction may not be the other end of the satisfaction continuum, since McCool and Peterson (1982) find that even visitors who have high levels of overall satisfaction sometimes report dissatisfaction with specific incidents during their visit. All of this calls for serious theoretical and methodological research on the satisfaction concept.

Carrying capacity research needs to expand its domain from current visitors to other populations. At this time, the norms of current visitors are used to define capacity. Other groups might include (1) past visitors who may have been crowded out; (2) future visitors who may be more or less tolerant of current use levels; and (3) potential visitors. Past visitors can be sampled from agency records if the information is kept, and nonvisitors can be sampled from general population surveys. Future visitors can be roughly identified from population trends and judgements about changes in demand. Sampling all three groups would obviously require a larger research budget.

The role of individual differences cannot be ignored. The approach taken in this book has been distinctly sociological, treating all visitors as equal. But it has been shown (Shelby et al. 1983) that individual variations in expectations and preferences influence perceived crowding. Other personal and social characteristics may produce different norms for identifiable subgroups. Recognizing these differences should be a continued effort in carrying capacity research.

There is much work to be done in developing more effective and less expensive methods for gathering data. Efforts to streamline research operations are reflected in the procedures described in this book, but opportunities still abound. In addition, agencies often have personnel who can devote some of their time to data-gathering. Because salaries, travel, and living expenses for field personnel usually represent a large part of a research budget, studies can be made much less expensive by enlisting agency or volunteer personnel. However, such personnel are usually untrained in research work, and they may have little personal stake in the project.

When should capacity studies be done? Use levels in some settings may already exceed social carrying capacity. In other cases, managers have little or no control over use levels; all they can do is to watch numbers increase and scramble to meet the demand. However, it may be useful to conduct studies even when social capacities have been exceeded or managers cannot control use levels. Few areas are full all of the time. By establishing capacities, managers can inform user groups about the times and locations when use level is below carrying capacity. Setting up a social carrying capacity forces managers to specifically define the kinds of experiences they are trying to provide and acquaints the public with the idea of limiting use to protect experiences. The area may be over capacity for the type of experience the manager is trying to provide, but under capacity for the type of experience some people are seeking. An explicit determination of capacity gets the issue in front of the public. For these reasons, it is useful to identify social carrying capacity even when it has been exceeded or when use level is not a management parameter.

Implementation

Research is often ignored in the policy-making process. This frustrates managers trying to squeeze results from tight budgets and researchers who write reports and journal articles hoping to improve the quality of management decisions. It is a long way from an initial problem statement through the research and policy processes to implementation of a workable management plan. At Grand Canyon this process is essentially complete, so the example is developed in detail in the following section to provide guidance for researchers and managers who want to avoid some of the pitfalls and see research translated into action.[2]

It is often assumed that policy decisions are made in a rational, linear way. Idealized conceptions of the decision process usually include identifying goals, developing alternatives, considering consequences, and making an optimal decision. But real world decisions seldom fit such an orderly model. Decision makers are usually faced with unclear and changing objectives, and information for developing alternatives is limited by time, money, and the individual's cognitive ability (March and Simon 1958). As a result, decisions are most often satisfactory rather than optimal.

Similarly, policy adjustments are incremental; changes are usually small relative to previous policies (Wildavsky 1964 and others). This concept argues that decision makers consider a limited number of alternatives which differ only incrementally from each other and from the *status quo* (Braybrooke and Lindblom 1963). Large-scale changes are discounted as politically unrealistic, and long-term goals are usually too remote to have much impact.

Only immediate consequences are assessed, and less tangible impacts are discounted. Braybrooke and Lindblom (1963) also suggest that goals are seldom considered apart from the means or resources available to reach them, so goals and means are probably developed simultaneously. Several theorists (e.g., Weiss 1977, Lindblom and Cohen 1979, Wildavsky 1979) differentiate rational analysis or intellectual cogitation from social or political interaction. Their conclusion is that effective problem solving necessarily recognizes and integrates both activities.

Where does research enter in? Information based on research is one of the rational or intellectual components of decision making, but results become part of a dynamic political process. Policy makers have ongoing relationships with information sources as diverse as administrators, politicians, journalists, interest groups, and social scientists, and the decision process is disorderly and iterative as well as intellectual and rational. Research is only one kind of input, and it may be used by policy makers for a variety of purposes besides rational analysis. These include delaying action, avoiding responsibility, discrediting an opponent or policy, gaining recognition for success, or gaining support for future programs (see Weiss 1977 for a discussion of these issues).

The factors affecting research utilization can be divided into two general categories. The first concerns scientific characteristics of the research itself, including methodological quality, relevance and timeliness of information, and strength of findings (Cox 1977, Rossi and Wright 1977, Hawkins et al. 1978). Scientists tend to focus on factors in this category, particularly methodological problems such as defining research issues, designing the study, and reporting results in terms which make sense to clients.

High quality is clearly necessary if research is to stand up in the public arena, but it does not insure that results will be used in decision making. Even good research is sometimes ignored, and the possible reasons for this fall into a second category of political factors affecting utilization. The word "politics" often has negative connotations, particularly among scientists. But politics is simply a matter of getting things done where people are involved, which means dealing with personalities, values, budgets, bureaucracies, regulations, laws, and conflicts between interest groups. Research application necessarily involves these factors.

Weiss and Bucuvalas (1980) suggest that decision makers assess research on both scientific and political merit. A "truth test" judges the work in terms of its relevance, quality, and conformity with the individual's own knowledge of the situation, while a "utility test" determines the work's relationship to existing policy and its implications for a course of action.

Problems and Controversy in Grand Canyon

River runners and managers alike were alarmed by rapid increases in use prior to 1972. The River Use Plan issued by the Park Service in December of

1972 addressed the problem of uncontrolled use. Commercial outfitters had been allotted 105,000 user-days for 1972, but had used only 89,000; they would be held for the next few seasons to this 16 percent reduction. In addition, however, the Use Plan called for a reduction to 55,000 user-days by the 1977 season.

This reduction appeared absolute and arbitrary, and it was highly controversial, particularly among river outfitters. In March of 1973, with the Use Plan only three months old, the Department of the Interior issued a statement which began by saying that, "The decision which has been made regarding limitations . . . on the Colorado River was not made hastily and without taking into account all relevant factors." The document indicated that further information about use levels was needed and several years would be required to collect it. Limiting use to 1972 levels was seen as an interim measure to protect the Canyon's environmental and social values while studies were conducted.

This created an unusually good opportunity for a carrying capacity study. The agency made a commitment to limiting use if necessary, which established such a policy as an option and asserted the legitimacy of the agency to make the choice. The interim freeze on use provided the time needed to study the issue. Managers had made a commitment to basing the final decision on newly acquired data. The parallel conflict over the Park Service's decision to phase out motorized travel on the river was for the next few years a more controversial issue, reducing political pressure on the carrying capacity problem. Early statements by the agency also began to establish the general goal of providing a wilderness experience on the river. All these factors increased the likelihood that research would be effective and useful.

The capacity study was conducted in 1974 and 1975, and the final study report to the Park Service was submitted in June of 1976. Reports of twenty-eight other studies were received at about the same time. These included an economic analysis of outfitting businesses; a campsite inventory; a study of trails; ecological/biological studies of streamside flora and fauna, human waste disposal, fish, and water quality; and studies of hydrology and erosion. The Park Service put together a synopsis summarizing the findings of the studies and began integrating results into a management plan.

A year and a half later, at the end of 1977, the Park Service issued a Draft River Management Plan (DRMP) and a Draft Environmental Statement. These documents included proposals for establishing a carrying capacity which were finalized in a Final Environmental Statement (FES) in July of 1979. The following information is drawn from all three documents.

The management plan first established the "product" to be provided. "The goals for management of the Colorado River in Grand Canyon will be to perpetuate the wilderness river-running experience and to attempt to mitigate the influences of man's manipulation of the river" (DRMP, p. 12).

The wilderness experience goal was supported by earlier documents, including the 1971 Draft and 1975 Final Master Plans for the park, input from public meetings, two surveys of river users, and the feelings of managers. The solidarity of wilderness as a goal was extremely important throughout the discussion and controversy which surrounded the development of the management plan. Managers referred to it continually, explaining how proposed policies fit with the management goal. If someone questioned a policy, they had to either show why it did not serve the goal or else question the goal itself.

Sometimes the wilderness goal was challenged. As one person testified in the public record, "The river offers unique and exclusive *scenery* and one of the outstanding whitewater *thrills* in the world. Just how wilderness and wilderness experience involving solitude or primitive experience gets into the situation escapes me. The public is entitled to every opportunity that can be provided to enjoy the views and thrills (Morley Hudson, FES, p. IX-147, emphasis his). The proposed use limits were obviously inappropriate to a "views and thrills" goal. But most people did agree with the goal of providing a wilderness experience. This does not mean that a case has not been or could not be made for views and thrills in other places or at other times. But for now there was a strong consensus that river trips in Grand Canyon should provide a wilderness experience.

The plan went on to consider the four types of capacity, at least implicitly.

Ecological capacity. Data demonstrated that Glen Canyon Dam had wrought the most dramatic changes in the river environment, but it was also clear that "physical and biological changes are occurring as a result of current [float trip] use" (DRMP, p. 12). The most interesting observation, however, was that "these changes are not necessarily a direct function of visitor use levels, but more importantly, of visitor use patterns and activities" (DRMP, p. 13). One party using inappropriate camping techniques (e.g. for waste disposal) had a greater impact than many parties using lower impact methods.

The conditions, then, violated Rule 1 for establishing capacity: there was little relationship between use level and the biological factors which needed managing, and lowering use would not necessarily lower impacts. The situation required other management parameters aimed more precisely at decreasing impact at present use levels. These included carry-out of human waste, eliminating wood-gathering for fires, establishing single trails to control and concentrate random patterns of foot traffic at attraction sites, eliminating congestion and dispersing visitors more evenly at attraction sites and camps, and establishing an education program to inform users of appropriate use practices.

These lessons from Grand Canyon appear to be generalizable. Biological impacts appear to be a function of *kind* of use rather than *amount* of use, and they can best be mitigated by manipulating or introducing management parameters other than use level (see Hendee et al. 1978: 175). The problem of multiple trailing is a good example. Even if increased numbers of people cause more damage, decreasing use would not necessarily solve the problem. The more efficient approach is to establish one hardened trail which is more convenient for users, thereby concentrating traffic in one suitable area. The established trail must, of course, fit with value judgments about what is appropriate for the experience (e.g., a highly developed paved trail with interpretive signs would probably be inappropriate for the wilderness river experience).

Facility capacity was considered but was not a major factor. The original concerns for limiting use had been heavily influenced by launch facility overload; the ranger at Lee's Ferry couldn't check out trips efficiently at peak use times, and users were getting in each other's way on the ramp. But distributing use more evenly for social reasons would solve most facility problems, so current developments appeared adequate. The education program aimed at mitigating biological impacts created some minor facility and staff problems. It required a place to hold the one-day training sessions for private trip leaders, a method for efficiently showing the brief audio-visual program on use practices to other private users and commercial passengers, and additional staff to conduct both programs. The plan also proposed additional on-river interpretation and enforcement, necessitating patrol rangers and river-running equipment. Again the experience in Grand Canyon seems to generalize to other settings; facility problems can usually be mitigated by adding facilities, increasing staff, or redistributing use to ease peak-load pressures.

Physical capacity. One of the alternatives considered in the decision process was to increase visitor use level to the absolute physical carrying capacity of the system. The physical capacity of the river was seen as limited by the availability of campsites, and the campsite inventory study had worked out a physical carrying capacity based on a computer simulation model. Using the norm of one party per beach and providing a 4 x 8 foot flat sleeping area for each person, each site was evaluated in terms of the largest group it could accommodate. The capacity for the river was then assessed. "Under a very tight scheduling system of launch days and times, campsite space assignments, structured river travel restrictions, time and area limitations at attraction sites, and a standardized trip length of twelve days, this alternative could . . . (result in) . . . an 85 percent increase in total visitors and a 242 percent increase in total user days" (FES, p. VIII-4).

In assessing the possible impacts of this alternative, biological and facility factors were considered first. But because kind of use has a greater effect than amount of use, ecological impacts were not a major limiting factor. Additional facilities and staff for educational and enforcement programs would be required, but again this was not a major stumbling block. The greatest impacts would be social. By standardizing trips, this alternative would "significantly reduce options for trip variety and experiences" (FES,

p. VIII-5). Strict scheduling would be required to reduce contacts, although they would still exceed current levels. This would result in actual congestion from encounters as well as psychological congestion from being on a timetable and knowing that other trips were close in front and behind.

Regimentation would also occur in other aspects of the trip. Off-river stops would be limited to three to four hours, off-river overnight trips would be eliminated, and attraction site use would probably be more concentrated in the easily accessible locations. In sum, "regimentation, scheduling, and lack of options would detract from the quality of the visitor's experience" (FES, p. VIII-5). The Canyon was physically capable of holding more people, but no one seemed particularly interested in the necessary trade-offs; capacity based solely on space limitations would not fit anybody's idea of a wilderness experience.

Social capacity. It was clear that most people thought of river trips in terms of wilderness, but what constitutes a wilderness experience? The river management plan described a wilderness trip as leisurely and relaxed, with time for off-river stops and hikes as well as enjoying the river itself, allowing close contact with the river-canyon environment without interference from other parties.

Research had shown that use was concentrated in both space and time. In terms of space, problems were most likely to occur in certain sections of the Canyon and at the most popular attraction sites. But use was also concentrated in time. The number of people launching each day averaged 130-140 on Monday and Friday. In addition, 87 percent of the use occurred in May, June, July, and August, 13 percent occurred in April and September, and there was virtually none the rest of the year.

The problem, then, was to choose a use level which would allow as many people as possible to use the resource without lowering the quality of the wilderness experience. The physical capacity option had been rejected because the necessary tight scheduling was seen as an infringement on the relaxed atmosphere required for a wilderness experience.

The solution was to lower use at peak times. Although this could be accomplished by decreasing the overall seasonal use level, a more efficient approach was to establish the daily launch limit which would produce contact levels in line with most people's preferences (three or fewer per day; see Chapter 5). It was then possible to lengthen the season so that this number of parties could leave on as many days as possible.

The plan called for a six-month summer season with a maximum of three trips leaving each day, and a six-month winter season with three trips leaving each week. The lower winter limit was intended to keep use levels low enough to allow the natural cleansing of beaches (research showed that heavily used beaches were cleaner in the spring than in the fall, although the biological process was not well understood). The winter season was also intended to "provide for a wilderness river trip where the likelihood of encountering other trips is remote" (FES, p. I-8). Although the primary justification for the lower winter level appeared to be biological, the plan provided for two kinds of experiences with different encounter levels. Providing these kinds of options was a real first in river management.[3]

The Final Environmental Statement discussed the impacts of the carrying capacity decision. The status of soils and vegetation, wildlife, water quality, air quality, and cultural resources would generally remain the same or improve as a result of new regulations regarding camp and practices. Social factors were the other major considerations. "With the more even dispersal of use during a longer season, daily and weekly launch schedules, and smaller party size, the number of contacts per day and the number of persons encountered off-river should be reduced. The visitors' river running experience, in terms of the amount of use encountered on the river, is expected to increase in quality" (FES, p. III-16).

The River Management Plan was finalized and approved in December of 1979. In November of 1980, before the plan's major provisions took effect, Senator Hatch from Utah attached a rider to the appropriations bill for the budget of the National Park Service for fiscal year 1981. Prompted by a small group of commercial outfitters disgruntled about certain aspects of the plan, the rider stated that "none of the funds appropriated in this Act shall be used for the implementation of any management plan for the Colorado River within the Grand Canyon National Park which reduces the number of user days or passenger launches for commercial motorized launches . . . for the preferred use period '' (the summer use season). The rider was passed, overturning parts of the planning process which had been going on since 1974 and had included considerable research, public involvement, political interaction, and compromise.

The so-called "Hatch Amendment" was primarily aimed at blocking the Park Service's attempt to phase out motorized river trips, but it also precluded the attempt to lower use in the summer months. The effect was to revert to the limit of 150 people per day established as part of the interim use limits in the early 1970s. With average trip sizes of fifteen to thirty, this would allow five to ten launches per day. Data showed that this would produce encounter levels greater than the preferences of most users, thus exceeding social carrying capacity.

Some Lessons in Research, Politics, and Decision Making

(1) Determining policy direction is an interactive process, so management goals should be stated as early as possible; information needs become more clear, and goals can be more thoroughly developed as managers interact with researchers, interest groups, and others. In Grand Canyon the wilderness experience goal was suggested somewhat tentatively in 1971 (perhaps as a political trial balloon). Succeeding documents restated and clarified the goal as public reaction and research results provided more

information. By the time final documents were written, the goal was clearly defined and well established. General goals are needed at the outset to determine the relevant areas for research and to inform the public. But as data become available, there will be more information about possibilities and public sentiment. Grand Canyon data helped clarify objectives for carrying capacity. There is a dynamic relationship between goals and policy formulation (Braybrooke and Lindblom 1963).

Stating management goals will also help focus the interactive process. Critics can disagree with goals, giving managers a chance to reconsider or modify their position or perhaps better defend it. Critics may also find themselves agreeing with general goals but disagreeing with the action chosen to reach them. This may encourage managers to think of more effective policies, or users may suggest alternatives of their own. Both these are more likely to create a situation where managers and users are working together to come up with the best solution; criticism is more likely to be constructive.

(2) As a corollary to (1) above, dialogue between managers and researchers is an essential part of the interactive process. For example, meetings with Park Service personnel and an annual Grand Canyon Research Symposium provided a number of opportunities for researchers to report preliminary findings. This encouraged them to organize their thoughts and allowed managers and others to see patterns emerge. All groups had numerous opportunities to identify unanticipated problems and take corrective action, and managers were able to learn about issues along with researchers. When final research reports were submitted there were more details but no major surprises. Interaction creates advocates for research within the agency.

Researchers often assume that their input is solely rational. The Grand Canyon example and other work (e.g., Wildavsky 1979) suggest that research must be combined with political interaction in the decision process. Controversial policies probably require support from both areas. The early decision to reduce use in Grand Canyon is a classic example where managers went beyond their data and/or their political support.

(3) Agencies can establish the ground rules regarding the use of scientific data. The Park Service did this (perhaps unwittingly) in the early stages at Grand Canyon by saying that carrying capacity decisions would take research results into account. The same thing happened later when allocation became an issue and private users insisted that sociological research be extended to include private trips. Rational analysis in the form of research was established as a legitimate part of the decision process, as was the agency's authority to make capacity decisions.

(4) A good information base requires an investment of time and money. The Colorado River Research Program for Grand Canyon took three years of intensive work on twenty-nine different studies at a cost of about $750,000. Areas lacking the national prominence of a place like Grand Canyon cannot

afford and may not need this kind of investment, but this often is used as an excuse for limited data, low quality information, and poorly founded decisions. Similarly, budget limitations create difficult situations for researchers, who must realistically assess how much can be done with the available resources. The procedures described in this book should help cut the costs of capacity studies, but good research is seldom cheap. Findings are more likely to be used if the agency has a real (i.e. monetary) investment in the research.

If policies are questioned, the investment in good information may save a great deal of time and money which would otherwise be spent defending and backtracking. At this point the methodological quality of the study and the strength of the findings are crucial, as Kilgore (1978) suggests. Researchers have an obligation to stand behind their work and explain or defend it, in court if necessary. This will obviously be difficult if the work is poor or conclusions have overstated the results.

(5) Research may serve purposes other than information gathering, as Weiss (1977) suggests. The research program in Grand Canyon bought three years of time to stabilize use under an interim management plan, and also provided an opportunity to define the issues and to consider solutions in a relaxed atmosphere. The issues were complex and all parties had a chance to become educated. It appears that these benefits were unanticipated, but policy makers aware of such possibilities may be able to capitalize on them.

(6) Social science data tend to represent the views of less vocal individuals or groups, and research results may be attacked by those who are more vocal. Grand Canyon data from public meetings and user surveys showed that most people supported the wilderness experience goal, but these findings were questioned by some outfitters whose views had previously carried greater weight. This is an example of a collective action problem; organized interests have powerful structural motivations to make their views known to policy makers, while more isolated individuals who make up the public at large are less likely to either speak up or speak forcefully. Publicly funded social science research is essentially a structural solution to make the quieter voices heard. Friesema and Culhane (1976) show that public comments on U.S. Forest Service Environmental Impact Statements act in a similar way; they better represent the views of nonbusiness interests than do district rangers' routine contacts.

(7) Timing is critical. Research should be done as early as possible, preferably before there is a problem. At the Grand Canyon, use level was frozen in 1972, and appropriate studies were completed before actual use had greatly exceeded capacity. On the Rogue, however, use levels had exceeded capacity by the time a study was done. No matter how clear the data, it is not possible to turn back the clock, and it appears politically impossible to substantially reduce use levels on the Rogue at this time. If people think a study is needed, it probably is. The greatest risk is that research will come too late.

(8) The most important lesson is that research can provide information to help managers make better decisions about carrying capacities. Some researchers have questioned the usefulness of the carrying capacity concept (Becker et al. 1984; Burch 1984; Wagar 1974). These criticisms focus on the problem of how science can help managers with the evaluative component of capacity decisions. Wagar (1974) points out that carrying capacity "suggests that the reasons for limiting use reside in the characteristics of a specific site and not in its contribution to human experiences." Defining "acceptable consequences" of particular use levels is a "value choice rather than a technical issue," and Wagar contends that carrying capacity decisions can only be made based on a conceptual framework which clearly acknowledges the role of value judgments.

The Grand Canyon example shows how evaluative information combines with descriptive data about the resource to help with management decisions. The encounter norms approach also shows how specific data from interest groups can be used to develop evaluative standards. To establish ecological capacity, a biologist might show managers how increasing visitor numbers affect the existence of a rare or endangered species. To establish social capacity at Grand Canyon, social science data showed how rapidly increasing use levels affected the existence of the rare wilderness experience available on the Colorado River. Managers acted to protect the opportunity for this experience, as they would to protect an endangered species. That the political maneuvering in the Hatch Amendment forced the Park Service to adjust capacity upwards may cause us to question the wisdom of the political process, but it does not decrease the usefulness of the carrying capacity concept or of scientific input into the decision-making process.

Notes

1. These observations were made during the summer of 1979. We would like to thank our students in a seminar "Social Carrying Capacity in Recreation Settings" for their assistance.

2. This section is drawn from papers by Shelby and Nielsen (1976a) and Shelby (1981b).

3. The plan also called for a phase-out of motorized trips and an increase in the amount of private use. These actions, like the carrying capacity decision, had major impacts on the river running scene. They are not discussed here except as they relate to the carrying capacity issue.

7—The Next Step: Allocating Use

Chapter Overview

Establishing carrying capacity may lead to an allocation problem; if demand consistently exceeds supply, then some sort of rationing system will be necessary. Such systems are based on goals such as equality (equal shares or equal chances), equity (unequal shares based on inputs), social efficiency (where those who value the experience most have priority), and recognizing the needs of particular user groups. Specific objectives for permit systems are derived from these goals.

There are five allocation mechanisms available to implement goals and objectives. **Pricing** leads to social efficiency but may favor those with more money and be politically and administratively unwieldy for some forms of public recreation. **Queuing** (first-come/first-served) seems fairer because time is more evenly distributed than money, but it favors local users and in some areas leads to inefficiencies and cheating. **Merit systems** eliminate the unqualified, but choosing the selection criteria is difficult.

Reservations are widely used for campground allocations, and they could be extended to other forms of recreation such as river running or hunting. Reservations place a premium on advance planning. They are costly, although costs can be passed along to users. On-site manual systems are slow and labor intensive, but they have a degree of flexibility. Computerized systems cost more to set up, but they run efficiently and allow those turned away at one site the opportunity to choose another. Reservation systems have problems with no-shows, although fees and overbooking appear to help.

Lotteries are often used for hunting permits, and could also be extended to other recreation activities. They are costly to run and require advance planning by users. The public generally perceives them as fair, but lotteries are often inefficient because those who value a recreation experience are often treated the same as casual applicants. However, it is possible to give groups such as landowners, residents, or previously unsuccessful applicants a higher probability of success. Lotteries can handle group applications, and no-shows can be reduced by charging application fees. It is also possible to design lottery systems to accommodate commercial guides or outfitters.

Allocation systems require tough decisions about goals and objectives. Management parameters are the alternative mechanisms described above, and impact parameters are the effects of each mechanism on various user groups in terms of costs, effort, and freedom of use. These impacts can be assessed in terms of evaluative standards developed from principles such as equality, equity, efficiency, and need. The time to think about allocation is *before* use in an area has reached carrying capacity. It helps to gather basic information about users so the impacts of a proposed system can be assessed objectively. Developing an allocation system should actively involve user groups.

The Next Step: Allocating Use

"Bake a pie, cut it into eight pieces, destroy two of the slices, and introduce ten people anxious to eat the remainder. As the pie lovers argue over whether to draw straws or divide the pie into crumb-size servings, triple the contestants and remove another three slices. What do you have? The story of America's wilderness." (Miller 1981)

This book has focused on carrying capacities. Capacities determine the size of the pie by specifying the number of people or groups that can use an area for a particular kind of experience. Limiting use resolves the capacity issue, but it opens the allocation issue, which is often sufficiently controversial that resource managers feel they have jumped out of the frying pan into the fire.

This chapter is a brief description of the uncharted territory facing managers who implement carrying capacities. It covers allocation principles and strategies and specifies the kinds of data that are useful for monitoring allocation systems. It does not explore the allocation issue as thoroughly as the first six chapters explored the capacity issue, because that would require another book, and more definitive studies have yet to be done. This chapter is drawn from a more detailed treatment specific to rivers (Shelby and Danley 1980).

The carrying capacity and allocation issues, although closely related, are distinct. Carrying capacity determines the appropriate number of people for a particular kind of experience; it involves setting a limit. Allocation distributes this limited number of opportunities among potential users; it means deciding who will use the resource when demand exceeds capacity. Because the use of rivers has increased so rapidly, allocation has become a controversial issue involving heated public debate, political maneuvering, and lawsuits. Allocation has been a less prominent problem with other forms of outdoor recreation, but that will probably change if use continues to increase in those areas.[1]

The most common criteria are equality, equity, need, and/or efficiency.

Equality

Equality means that individuals have the same right to certain benefits. There are two ways of achieving equality: (1) give everyone an equal share;

or (2) give everyone an equal chance to obtain benefits. Suppose that six people on a river trip are sharing one six-pack of beer. The first form of equality would give each person a can. Now suppose there are seven people on the trip. Rather than dividing the six cans seven ways, people might draw straws, guess numbers, or use some other mechanism which gave each person an equal chance to win but awarded a whole can of beer to the winners. Similarly, we might have six hunters and six hunting permits. "Equal shares" equality would give each person one permit, while "equal chance" equality might assign each person a number from 1 to 6, roll a die, and give the winner all six permits. Where benefits are divisible, the first form of equality is usually used; where benefits are not divisible (as when twenty-seven persons compete for one permit), the second is probably preferred (Pauly and Willet 1972). Below is a goal and possible objectives for an allocation system based on equality.

Goal: Equality. *Everyone gets an equal share of the resource, or has an equal likelihood of getting to use it.*

Possible objectives: *Give equal shares or equal opportunities by one or more of the following:*

(1) Seeing that no one gets to use the resource more often than anyone else.

(2) Giving everyone an equal probability of getting a permit, regardless of past success, need, value placed on using the resource, willingness to pay, type of trip desired (private or commercial), etc.

(3) Charging all users the same fees.

(4) Requiring everyone to use the same procedure for getting a permit.

(5) Reducing conflict by minimizing differences in the ways different user groups are treated.

Equity

Equality is not always "fair," so in some situations people resort to unequal but presumably more fair allocation norms. Equity is a term with several meanings, but in allocation it refers specifically to fairness. This has most often been defined as the ratio of inputs to outcomes for each individual (Walster et al. 1973). The contention is that if inputs are unequal then outcomes should be proportionately unequal. For the people on a river trip, equity might mean dividing the beer (outcome) in proportion to the amount of money contributed by each individual (input), rather than giving everyone the same amount. Equitable distribution is often more complex than equal distribution because there are many dimensions for measuring both inputs and outcomes. For example, it appears inequitable that resident Alaskans pay $25 for a brown bear tag while nonresidents pay $250. But residency connotes additional inputs (such as taxes), and nonresidents may place a higher value on the right to hunt (increasing their outcomes). The following is an example of an equity goal and related objectives.

Goal: **Equity**. *Those who put more into the system (money, time, effort, etc.) get more out of the system (e.g., greater likelihood of using the resource).*
Possible objectives: *Give a better chance of obtaining a permit to groups such as:*

    (1) Taxpayers or residents.
    (2) Those who have been unsuccessful at getting a permit in the past.
    (3) Those who are willing to pay higher permit fees.
    (4) Those who are willing to spend more time applying.
    (5) Those who have acquired specialized skills or equipment.
    (6) Those who have used the resource more in the past.
    (7) Those willing to donate time and effort (e.g., restoration or hauling trash).
    (8) Those who abide by regulations (e.g., those who show up to claim reservations, follow use practices, etc.)

Need

Recognizing need is another way of trying to assure fair rather than equal distribution. In dividing beer on the river, some people may "need" more to quench their thirst or to put them in a relaxed state of mind. Giving larger shares of food to people who are larger, more active, or more hungry is another obvious example, and in game management some permit systems give priority to subsistence hunting. Similarly, landowners are often given special access privileges when private land is surrounded by federal land. Need is often disregarded in favor of equality or equity because need is difficult to define.

Goal: **Recognize need**. *Give more to those who need more.*
Possible objectives: *Allow greater access to groups such as:*

    (1) Those owning land along or near a river.
    (2) Those who depend on a resource for their livelihood (such as fishermen or outfitters).
    (3) Public service organizations (such as boy scouts, remedial or correctional programs).

Social Efficiency

Social efficiency is maximized when a resource is put to its most highly valued use. Some people really like beer, for example, while others would rather drink river water. In this case, it is not socially efficient to divide the beer equally. Similarly, fine peeler logs can be used for firewood, but it is more efficient to use them for making plywood because we can substitute less valuable resources for use as firewood. Tastes in recreation vary, and people value different experiences differently. Some might be willing to give up golf, skiing, fishing, desserts, and a $1,000 bill to run a particular river, while others would just as soon visit Disneyland, climb a mountain, or watch a stock car race. If the goal is to maximize efficiency, use should be shifted to those who value the recreation experience the most. The obvious problem lies in determining value.

Goal: Maximize social efficiency. *Produce maximum benefits by seeing that the resource is used by those for whom it has the greatest value.*

Possible objectives: *Require users to assess the value of using a particular resource relative to the value of other desirable activities by giving the permit a "cost" in terms of:*

(1) Money for permit fees.
(2) Time and effort required to carry out application procedures.
(3) Planning in advance of the time when use will occur.
(4) Skills or equipment required to use the resource.

These costs might be: (*a*) equal for all users or (*b*) different for different users, giving those willing to "pay" more a greater likelihood of getting a permit.

To summarize, equality, equity, need, and social efficiency are all important factors in resource allocation. Equality is probably the simplest criterion; it simply requires equal opportunity or equal outcome. Equity, need, and efficiency are more complex because they require some means of assessing costs and benefits (value) for different individuals. In market economics, value is expressed in monetary terms, although economists recognize that dollars may have different values for different people, depending on how much money they have. The assessment of value becomes increasingly difficult with nonmarket commodities such as recreation. Here the criteria for comparing values may include money, time, opportunities foregone, the effort invested in acquiring skills or equipment, or the availability of substitute activities. The complexity of these factors makes equitable and efficient allocation quite difficult. There are also trade-offs in moving from one criterion to another, which increases the difficulty of deciding on a principle or combination of principles. Past research suggests that equity is preferred when production or efficiency is the goal, while equality is stressed when units of comparison are unclear or when the goal is to reduce conflict (Deutsch 1975, Leventhall 1976).

Allocation Systems

There are five basic strategies for allocating scarce resources: pricing, queuing, merit, reservation, and lottery.[2] Pricing, queuing, and merit are discussed briefly because managers seem unlikely to choose them for allocating backcountry resources. Reservation and lottery systems are discussed in greater detail because they have been used to allocate campground access and hunting permits in many states, and they are often proposed for managing rivers or backcountry areas. Most allocation systems combine one or more of these five mechanisms.

Pricing

When the demand for something exceeds the available supply it is a simple matter to increase the price until demand equals supply. Pricing is commonly used to allocate market commodities such as diamonds or gasoline. In the case of recreation, supply is often limited to the administratively defined carrying capacity. In general, pricing would mean charging a fee at least during times when demand exceeded capacity. The fee would have to be high enough to cause those less willing or less able to pay to drop out of the market, decreasing demand until it equaled supply.

Pricing has several advantages. It encourages people to prioritize their desires; recreation experiences are (apart from the effects of income inequalities) distributed to those who value them the most (resulting in equity and efficiency); and demand is automatically balanced with available supply. Pricing would eliminate artificially low (zero) prices which encourage those who place little value on an experience to compete with people for whom the experience is important. Pricing might also allow those who use the resource to pay for it, rather than having all taxpayers subsidize the recreation pursuits of special interest groups.

There are also disadvantages of pricing. Efficiency may not be maximized because income is unevenly distributed; pricing discriminates against those who are unable to pay as well as those who are unwilling, and a person with little money who places a high value on a particular experience might be squeezed out by a casual participant with a higher income. However, the cost of a permit would probably be low in relation to expenses for equipment, food, travel, and time and opportunity costs, and people who could afford these other costs could probably afford a permit.

Managers of the recreation areas we have studied seem reluctant to consider pricing as a mechanism for limiting use, although this appears to be changing. Pricing is most commonly used to allocate privately held resources. Common property or public resources are less likely to be marketed, especially when the managing entity does not have clear guidelines for pricing or marketing. Public recreation resources are usually nonmarket commodities, although one can think of examples where contracts allow marketing (ski areas on public land) or where fees are charged in a quasimarket (public campgrounds).

Pricing is simple and well understood. But it is difficult to defend as long as income is unequally distributed. If the resource is to benefit all citizens, why should the public have to pay a fee high enough to turn people away? A fee of $50 to $100 per person might reduce demand for river trips in Grand Canyon, and it has been argued that outfitters control demand for commercial trips through pricing (Shelby and Danley 1979). But as a society we seem committed to the idea that access to public lands should be distributed at little or no charge, and this view blinds us to the fact that access rights to some areas (particularly western whitewater rivers) have acquired considerable monetary value (Shelby 1984). It may be time to seriously consider pricing mechanisms for backcountry areas, at least during peak use periods.

Queuing

Queuing means waiting in line or first-come/first-served. It is similar to pricing, but time rather than money is traded for the desired commodity. Queues are commonly used for admission to popular shows, sports events, or concerts, usually in combination with pricing. Queues have been used in backcountry permit systems, either for some percentage of use or for unclaimed reservations.

The advantage of queuing is that, like pricing, it allows individuals to assess the value of the resource in relation to their willingness to pay in terms of time waiting in line. Some argue that allocation by time is the most fair because time is evenly distributed; we all have 24-hour days. But there are also disadvantages to queuing. Time is worth a great deal to those with structured and busy lives, but has relatively less value for those with fewer demands; queuing therefore discriminates against those whose time is precious. Many backcountry areas are in remote areas, so queues for permits might cause other problems. If queues occurred on the day of departure, parties with a full load of gear might drive hundreds of miles and then be denied access, producing angry visitors and encouraging cheating. If the queue happened in advance, people would have to make two trips. Queuing might also require facilities and administration for the people waiting in line (an added expense), and time spent waiting is lost for everyone whereas a monetary fee becomes a gain for whoever collects it.

Merit

A merit system would distribute permits on the basis of some demonstrable skill, knowledge, personal attribute, or past behavior. This is a relatively untried option in recreation, but qualifying-exams for government employees, safety courses for hunters, or tests for drivers provide some examples from other areas. Demonstration of competence is already required on some rivers, though as a safety precaution rather than an allocation mechanism.

Merit tends to be used for establishing minimum qualifications rather than for choosing from a surplus of qualified persons. The ability to eliminate the unqualified appears to be its primary advantage, although the time, effort, and money spent acquiring merits would encourage users to assess the value of the experience and might increase social efficiency. Requiring merit beyond minimum qualifications creates serious difficulties in deciding on criteria. Add to this the problems of subjective judgment, favoritism, and possible black markets, and administration might be a nightmare.

Reservation

The notion of making a reservation is familiar to most of us. Spaces in airplanes, trains, hotels, and restaurants are often reserved through world-wide computer networks, although many reservations are handled by simpler systems. All reservation systems have one common effect: they place a premium on advance planning. Reservations favor users who can and do plan ahead, and the emphasis on planning distinguishes reservations from other rationing techniques.

Reservations have been used for a variety of public recreation resources, but campgrounds are probably the best and most thoroughly documented example. Site-specific, manually operated systems were first used in the Northwest in the late 1940s (Burnett 1973). Many still operate on the same basis, while others have developed into state-wide computerized networks.

Manual systems allow users to specify individual sites, provide direct contact between users and managers, and probably favor local users. Referrals are limited within the system, data collection and analysis are cumbersome, and more labor is required than with automated systems. Although manual systems are the most frequently used, they often fail to keep pace with changing conditions or agency goals, and may be eventually replaced by automated programs.

Computerized systems usually require a larger initial capital investment, but they are less labor-intensive once in operation. They provide efficient referral services and easy data collection and analysis. However, there is usually no direct visitor contact with the campground which reduces planning flexibility and may lead to misunderstandings.

No-shows. One of the drawbacks of the reservation mechanism is that people speculate about their use of a service in the future. Because the costs of making a reservation are usually low, people often reserve a spot even if they may not claim it; the resulting no-shows can be a real management problem, particularly in campgrounds where unclaimed spots may be visible to those arriving without reservations.

There are several ways to raise the cost of not claiming a reservation, but deposits and advance payment of fees are the most common. The Ticketron/ American Express systems require that users pay in advance the entire camping fee plus a reservation fee. If the reservation is cancelled prior to the first day of a reservation period, the camping fee is refunded; if cancellation occurs later, part or all of the fee is forfeited. In any case, a cancellation fee (usually equal to the reservation fee) is deducted from the refund. The same principle is used in manual reservation systems.

Data regarding the effectiveness of prepayments are not conclusive. It seems reasonable that no-show rates would be lower if (1) cancellation is easy for the user; and (2) substantial prepayment is required. The American Express system used by the Park Service in 1973 offered easy cancellation and refunds to no-shows, while the Oregon 1977 manual system offered easy cancellation prior to the reservation period but no refunds for no-shows. Oregon's no-show rate was slightly lower (at 11 percent) than American Express's 14.8 percent (National Park Service 1974, Whitam 1978). The size of the prepayment also appears to affect no-show rates. Midway through the 1972 camping season, Congress eliminated camping fees in most federal campgrounds. A survey of the National Park reservation system that year indicated that no-shows and cancellations were substantially higher after fees were eliminated (Magill 1976). This suggests that deposits and prepayment, which are essentially pricing mechanisms, might be effective. Most agencies are reluctant to levy such fees because they are hard to handle administratively.

A relatively unexplored technique for reducing no-shows is to penalize habitual offenders by denying them future permits. One system attempting this kind of control is in the North Carolina State Parks, where users are permitted only two cancellations or no-shows per year (Stevens 1978). Computerized systems could do audits for habitual no-shows, but Ticketron, for one, does not collect users' names. The American Express system did collect users' names, but no-show audits were not made during the program's one-year history (National Park Service 1974, Magill 1973).

Airlines and hotels often make reservations for more spaces than they have available. The idea is to compute average no-show rates on the basis of past behavior and then take reservations that far beyond capacity. Reservation systems which record user characteristics might also use differential overbooking, a technique which discriminates according to the past performance of different groups. Hotel reservation networks have found, for example, that business travelers are less likely to honor reservations than are families, and the system compensates by overbooking business travelers at a correspondingly higher rate (Anonymous 1974). Although such practices have caused trouble for airlines recently, campgrounds might be better suited to overbooking because most systems withhold a percentage of sites in order to allow for adjustments. No-show rates for different categories of campers could be monitored for a season or two, analyzed, and used to establish overbooking rates. Evidence suggests that no-show rates vary according to the reservation method (by mail, phone, or through ticket agencies), and keeping records on other categories of campers might add to this knowledge (National Park Service 1974, Burnett 1973).

Costs of reservation systems. Reservation systems are expensive. Even the smallest program requires labor, equipment, and office space. Whether these costs are absorbed in the operating budget of the agency and passed on to taxpayers, or whether those using the service pay, costs cannot be ignored.

Park agencies are increasingly likely to pass on the costs of reservation systems to users, either directly or through contractors such as Ticketron. Even some decentralized systems charge $1.00 (Utah) to $3.00 (Michigan and New Jersey) per reservation. All contracted or computerized systems levy a reservation fee ranging from $1.50 (New York) to $1.75 (California and Virginia). These charges provide vendor profit, but do not always pay the agency's expenses, even though some contracts allow the state to receive a portion of the reservation fee.

Lottery

Lotteries are a frequently mentioned but poorly understood allocation mechanism. In the context of this discussion, a pure lottery refers to the random, unbiased selection of applicants, where each individual has an equal probability of being selected (an example of the "equal chance" method of achieving equality). Using randomization to make social choices has been called "eminently fair" by some (Hardin 1969) and "a denial of rationality... and a denial of man's humanity" by others (Wolfle 1970). The random selection of game permits is a well-established application of lotteries in recreation, so it will be explored in some detail here.

Most states charge for game permits, so limited market mechanisms operate in many systems. But game permit fees are usually well below the market price. Exceptions include a big game permit fee in Alaska, which often exceeds $100, with a maximum fee for a musk ox permit at $1,000. Fees of this magnitude obviously help limit the number of applications (Alaska 1977), but pricing does not necessarily insure a reasonable hunter turnover because wealthy persons are continuously favored by this form of rationing. Alaska waives resident fees upon demonstration of financial need, however.

Game lotteries vary tremendously from state to state; they are used to handle anywhere from 1,000 applications for three hunts on the Catahoula National Wildlife Refuge in Louisiana (Joyner 1977) to 350,000 applications for 273 hunts in Wyoming (Rinehart 1977).

Most agencies handling a low number of hunts draw successful applicants by hand. As the number of permits and hunts increase, states tend to automate or computerize their systems to handle the increased data. The decision to computerize usually depends on some kind of cost/benefit analysis. Some benefits of computerization are: a broader, more complete data base; an automatic check for compliance with regulations and edit for applicant errors; automatic selection, billing, and permit mailing; automatic printing for lists and reports; and savings in time and possibly money. Idaho's Fish and Game Department analyzed their computerized system, which handles about two hundred hunts and 90,000 applications. The system cost $16,000 to design and 24 cents to 27 cents to process each application (Clapsaddle and Greenley 1979).

Equity and equality. Lotteries usually handle equity and equality by establishing classes, adjusting turnover rates, and permitting group applications. A pure lottery would allow all individuals, regardless of circumstance, an equal chance of selection for any given hunt. This kind of total equality is not usually preferred in hunting because residents, landowners, and some other priority classes are often given preference. Priority is handled through separate drawings for each class. For example, in the Nevada buck-deer hunt, nonresidents are given only 10 percent of the permits. Other states (e.g., Montana, New Mexico) recognize landowner priority in addition to residency. Variations range from no preference for in-state hunters (e.g., Oregon) to exclusion of nonresidents from lotteries (e.g., British Columbia, Utah).

Persons who were unsuccessful in previous drawings are often given preferences in subsequent drawings. The idea is to insure that all who apply for a particular permit will eventually get one, so some of the chance is removed from an otherwise random draw in order to maintain a turnover of hunters. This is usually done in one of two ways: previously successful applicants are denied permits for a certain number of years (ranging from one year to a lifetime), or unsuccessful applicants participate in a precedence drawing based on the number of accumulated unsuccessful applications (Sandfort 1977, Oregon 1977).

Social groupings. Game agencies recognize that social aspects of hunting are important and that hunting without partners may be dangerous. Therefore, most states issue lottery-drawn permits to groups as well as individuals. The most common example is the two-person application. Other variations include groups up to six persons (e.g., Wyoming) and an unlimited number of persons per group (e.g., Nevada deer permits). In all drawings where group applications are accepted, each group is treated as one selection number; if that number is chosen by the draw, all persons in the group receive permits.

Each group, regardless of its size, has an equal chance of being selected. When group size can vary, there is a risk of exceeding the draw quota by the number of persons in the group. Two procedures are used to deal with this. For hunts where the total number of permits is critical, group size is often restricted to two or even one. The other procedure simply programs the computer to stop when the number of selected permits is equal to the draw quota minus the maximum group size allowed (Arizona 1977).

Efficiency and no-shows. Efficiency in game permit allocation is partially served by pricing and the time spent in application procedures. Beyond that, agencies try to provide information which allows hunters to assess their chances of obtaining any given permit. Due to the uneven distribution of animals and hunting pressure, game agencies divide states into game management units. Prior to each hunt, managers decide how many permits to issue for each management unit. These quotas are published in controlled hunt regulations along with descriptions of the areas and the length of the hunts. Hunters can then consider their area preferences in light of permit quotas. Hunters may also indicate second or third choices so that unsuccessful applicants can be referred to units with remaining permits. This system allows hunters to maximize individual preference and helps to distribute hunting pressure more uniformly. Unfortunately, game agencies usually publish only the quota and not the probability of success in the draw, so hunters base their decisions on incomplete information.

Alaska's McNeil River Game Preserve permits represent an interesting alternative, where applicants are given information about their chances of obtaining different kinds of permits. Permits allow users to take photographs in areas frequented by brown bears in early summer. The goals of the permit system are to maximize public use within capacity constraints during the regulatory period and to manage for wilderness values with only minimal development (Faro 1974). Permits are for one or five days, and the Alaska Fish and Game Department publishes the probability of receiving each type of permit based on previous seasons' data. Individuals can make a decision based on desired date, length of permit, and the chances of selection. As with other game permits, first, second, and third choices are allowed to distribute and maximize use. Even though permits are selected at random, individuals can exercise some control and thereby increase efficiency.

One of the problems with lotteries is that hunters often apply for as many tags as possible, whether they intend to use them or not. To reduce frivolous applications, some states charge a nonrefundable application fee for each lottery. These fees range from $1.00 in Idaho and Montana to $10.00 in Alaska (musk ox). Other states (e.g., New Mexico) place limits on the number of lottery hunts one can apply for. Issuing more permits than the optimum is another way of dealing with no-shows, a system which works well when a slight over- or under-harvest is not critical. Another method of handling no-shows is to issue unclaimed permits on a first-come/first-served basis. This favors local and spontaneous use, but it could be difficult to adopt on large hunts (Joyner 1977).

Game lotteries and commercial guides. It is difficult to determine the effects of lotteries on guides because there have been no systematic data collection efforts. The following is based on informal discussions with game managers and a few guides. It is relevant to other forms of recreation where guides are used (such as river running).

States with a high ratio of guides to hunters have experienced difficulty with lottery drawings (e.g., Wyoming, Alaska, Montana, and Colorado). The most frequently mentioned problem is that guides do not have enough time between the drawing and the hunt to schedule trips. The other common complaint is that guides relying on return business cannot serve past clients who have been unable to get permits.

State agencies seem to take one of five positions on this issue: (1) Let the guides handle the situation as best they can (e.g., Wyoming and Colorado). (2) Give the guides some kind of prearranged percentage of the permits.

Alaska does this indirectly with some hunts by giving a high percentage of permits to nonresidents, who tend to seek guiding services (Rausch 1977). (3) Release to interested guides the names of successful applicants so they can be contacted. States normally charge a nominal fee to cover costs (e.g., Idaho, Nevada). (4) Increase the time between drawing and hunt, giving guides more planning time (e.g., New Mexico). (5) Require nonresident hunters to obtain a guide. Nonresident guiding requirements were used until recently in Colorado, Wyoming, and Montana, but all have retracted them because nonresident hunters found the laws too restrictive and/or because courts found them unconstitutional. British Columbia has retained the nonresident guiding requirements, but the lottery-drawn hunts are currently closed to nonresidents. Of these alternatives, guides understandably prefer their own quotas rather than the risk of not obtaining clients after a lottery.

Guides seem to recognize the need for control of hunting and guiding, but disagree about the methods which best accomplish this. Communication between guides and agencies often appears to be poor, and guides' comments are directed at poor planning or unclear goals rather than at the lotteries themselves. Certainly outfitters deserve consideration, although agency goals and user needs may conflict with those of guides.

Nonrationing Methods: Less Restrictive Measures
There are a variety of ways to reduce congestion or crowding without actually rationing use, some of which were discussed earlier in this book. Most problems are caused by concentrations of use, either in time (days of the week, months of the season, etc.) or space (launch areas, attraction sites, etc.). Mechanisms which distribute use more evenly will increase the available supply of space.

Such mechanisms are extremely valuable for increasing utilization and gaining political acceptance. There are limitations, however. These mechanisms require use permits, so physical, ecological, and social carrying capacities will still have to be carefully considered. In addition, redistribution of use is only a temporary solution. If demand continues to increase, it is only a matter of time before capacity is again reached. Allocation will be necessary at that point so the issue will only have been postponed.

Developing New Allocation Systems
The general framework outlined in Chapter 1 can be applied to allocation as it can to most resource management decisions. Management parameters include alternative mechanisms such as pricing, queuing, merit, reservation, and lottery. Impact parameters are the effects on user groups in terms of the cost and effort involved, the probability of getting permits, and the freedom with which they can be used. These impacts can be assessed in

terms of evaluative standards developed from principles such as equality, equity, efficiency, need, and other more specific allocation goals.

Allocation only becomes an issue when the number of people wanting to use an area exceeds carrying capacity. If an area does not have an established use limit, or if use pressures do not exceed the limit at least some of the time, then there is not yet an allocation problem. This does not preclude permits as a way of documenting use; it just means that rationing is not yet necessary.

Not having a problem now does not mean there will not be one in the future. The past fifteen years have seen rapid increases in the use of whitewater rivers, for instance, sometimes as great as 50-60 percent per year. If use might approach capacity in the foreseeable future, now is the time to think about allocation. It is always easier to set capacities or make allocation decisions before acceptable limits have been reached, and the development of a comprehensive scheme at the start is preferable to the establishment of unsatisfactory piecemeal solutions later.

Deciding on goals for an allocation system is a difficult but crucial task. Legal guidelines, agency mandates, court rulings, and the concerns of different interest groups all have to be considered. Equity, equality, efficiency, and recognizing need are frequently mentioned goals for allocation, but the objectives of groups such as outfitters, private users, and managers may differ sharply (Shelby and Danley 1980). It is useful to start out by actually listing the goals which seem appropriate. Each goal should then be defined with more specific objectives. This process often uncovers conflicts or inconsistencies which need to be resolved.

The next step is to consider different alternatives for accomplishing allocation objectives. Many systems combine different mechanisms. Try to specify the impacts of each alternative so they can be evaluated against your allocation goals. It helps to develop scenarios, starting with the visitor who wants a permit and ending with that visitor actually using the area. Major issues include handling requests for information, making the reservation (in person, by phone, by mail), handling applications (by hand or automation), issuing permits (by mail, at the launch site, etc.), necessary personnel and facilities (both office and field), costs, handling mistakes, and the problems of converting from an old to new system.

The system needs to be monitored on a long-term basis to see that it continues to meet allocation goals. The goals themselves may also change in time. Record keeping and data analysis are quite easy with a properly designed computerized system, but handkept records should not be too much of a burden if the process is carefully thought out. We suggest collecting the information described in Appendix 3 each year, even if you decide to stick with your present system. Uniform data collection is necessary for planning and evaluating any allocation system.

Notes

1. See the proceedings of the National Conference on Allocation of Recreation Opportunities on Public Land (Buist 1981) for a sampling of the issues and controversies.

2. This section draws heavily on Stankey and Baden's (1977) work on rationing backcountry use.

Appendix 1
Measurement for Capacity Studies

Use Levels

Developing Use Measures

To accurately represent use levels, three components need to be considered: location, unit of use, and period of time. For example, use level can be defined as, "The number of people using the ski lifts (unit of use) at Bachelor Butte (location) each week (period of time)." For each component, think about the way the area is used, and select units which reflect use patterns and are reasonably efficient to administer.

To specify *location*, identify geographic areas where use occurs. Attractions such as lakes, rivers, or mountains are common focal points. With these established, map the points where users enter the system. Include officially designated accesses such as boat ramps, road ends, and trail heads, as well as *de facto* accesses established by users. This may be a simple task, as it was with the single access point at Lee's Ferry in Grand Canyon, or it may be more complex, as with the multiple access points used by floaters on the Brule or deer hunters in Wisconsin. If areas within the study location are substantially different in location or character, it may be necessary to keep separate figures.

With areas identified, decide on *units* for measuring use. One obvious alternative is to count people, as we did in the managed goose hunt and on the Rogue river. This unit has intuitive appeal, and it may have been used for data collection in the past. Other units, however, may be more convenient or useful. In Grand Canyon, the Park Service originally tried to limit the number leaving Lee's Ferry to 150 people per day. The problem was that this required outfitters to guess in advance the number of passengers on a trip and then to notify the agency of any changes; this naturally became an administrative headache for everyone. And the number of passengers really did not make much difference. The reasons for limiting use—confusion at the launch site and congestion on the river—were more a function of the number of parties than the number of people. Crowding within groups, which was a function of the number of individuals, was controlled by establishing maximum party sizes.

The firing line goose hunt provides another example of differing units for amount of use. Everyone arrived by automobile and parked in the same place, so a count of cars in the lot (which was easier than counting people) was a reasonable reflection of people in the area. It is important to be flexible in thinking about the units to be counted, choosing a measure which is reasonably convenient and which accurately reflects use in the designated area. In most cases, it is possible to convert one unit to another. In the firing line hunt, for example, there was an average of 1.5 hunters per car, so either figure (people or cars) could be obtained from the other.

Time is the third component of a use level measure. We measured trips per week in Grand Canyon but visitors per day elsewhere; why the difference? The selection of a time frame depends on the cyclical variations of use (e.g. hourly, daily, etc.) as well as other factors such as the distances covered, travel speeds, and overall lengths of trips. In Grand Canyon, we began by measuring trips departing each day, but this measure showed little correlation with downstream encounters. Use levels were affected by launch numbers over several days. The solution was to measure use levels as trips per week, combining use on the launch date with that which occurred the three days before and after.

In summary, use level measures specify visitor numbers in a particular location, which may include entry points, focal points, or entire areas. They involve a particular unit, such as the individual person, the party, or a vehicle such as a car or a boat. Finally, there is a time dimension. This may be as long as weeks or as short as a day or even an hour. There are no hard and fast rules here because each setting is different. The best strategy is to obtain multiple measures and look for the most effective ones in the analysis.

Establishing Variation in Use

In order to determine the relationship between use level and contacts, use level must vary. If exactly one hundred people enter a given area every day, it is not possible to determine what might happen when ten or two hundred people visit the area. Variation in use usually occurs naturally, and it is possible to design a study to take advantage of this. River use in the Grand Canyon, for example, was concentrated in a summer season (May-August). High-use data were gathered in June, moderate-use data in early May and late August, and low-use data in April and September. On the Brule River, high use occurred on weekends and low use on weekdays.

There are two problems with natural variation. The first is that the type of trips and people on them may be different during the high and low use periods. Trips at different points in the use cycle may travel at a different pace, offer different prices, or select people with special interests, atypical life styles, or different kinds of vacation constraints. In Grand Canyon, for example, some outfitters offer longer "hikers' special" trips early in the season. These trips may be half again as long as standard trips, and they are run on a different schedule. It is reasonable to assume they appeal to a clientele with more time and higher activity levels. On the Brule River it is likely that locals use the river more on weekdays, which happens to be the low-use period. Low use for deer hunting occurred in northern Wisconsin, and the north differs from the south in many ways besides density. The seriousness of these kinds of differences depends on the nature of the study. Structural differences such as changed trip schedules or travel patterns should be recorded as variables because these may be important impacts of different amounts of use. Differences in visitor characteristics will only be problematic if these interact with other important variables such as perceptions or evaluations. Short of randomly assigning people to trips, areas, or days, the best solution is to measure visitor characteristics such as prior experience, vacation times, planning horizons, and flexibility and then control them statistically during analysis.

The other problem with natural variation is that it may not be great enough. Carrying capacity studies are usually undertaken only after use has become an issue; it is hard to get funding from agencies to study "underused" areas. Interim use limits have sometimes been established, which means that low and high use periods may not be available without at least temporarily lowering and/or raising the limit. Such changes may meet with political opposition.

The Grand Canyon study illustrates a particularly frustrating situation. The low-use period was no problem because off-season use was minimal. A higher than normal use period was needed to determine impacts associated with natural growth projections, but the Park Service had already instituted limitations on higher levels of use. A brief one- to two-week period of higher density was requested to see what the effects would be. Although the park superintendent had earlier endorsed the idea of such experimentation, the river manager was committed to his limits and never officially opened up a high-use period. Several months of negotiation with the Washington, D.C. office produced an experimental high-density period, but use was not as high as researchers would have liked. Whenever possible, then, temporary changes to explore and document the extremes of high and low use should be built into carrying capacity studies. But do not expect this to be easy.

Encounters

Developing Encounter Measures

Encounter measures, like density measures, have location, unit, and time components. Encounters occur in a variety of *locations*, including the river or trail, visitor attractions, camp areas, etc. Contacts may be concentrated in some rather than all of these areas, and the literature suggests that contacts occurring in some areas may have greater impact than those in others. As a result, it is usually desirable to develop separate measures describing each location.

There was some difficulty specifying locations on the Rogue River because managers were not familiar with attraction sites. The solution was to ask observers to keep records of all stops, and later compile a list of all the places visited by sampled trips. The percentages of trips stopping at each one gave an indication of those most often used. A similar approach can be used to identify popular campsites.

Comparisons among the study areas show that encounter *units* differ. On the Colorado and Rogue rivers each party was counted as one contact; groups tended to travel together, and one was usually well separated from the next. It made sense to count encounters as the number of parties seen even though one group in Grand Canyon might have from fifteen to forty people and the number of boats might vary from one to ten.

An encounter has different characteristics in other areas. On the Brule, tubers and fishers were generally met individually, so the encounter unit was a single person. Canoers came in pairs, two to a boat, so here canoes were counted. Hunters generally arrive in groups but then split up in the woods or along the firing line, so the number of individual hunters seen was used as the encounter measure.

Finally, encounter measures also have a *time* component. The first aspect of this is the period during which contacts occur. This is usually measured as encounters per day, even on multi-day trips. The other aspect is the length of the encounter. An average encounter on the Colorado or the Rogue lasted 10-15 minutes, while a hunter on the firing line was in sight of most other hunters in the area for the entire time he hunted (usually 2-3 hours). The time component selected should be consistent with the way encounters are experienced from the user's point of view.

The problem of measuring encounters is further complicated by the *type* of encounter; some contacts have unique characteristics which makes their impact on other users greater. Lucas (1964) showed that encounters with motorboats had a far greater impact on paddling canoers than did encounters with other canoes, and other studies show similar differences. Similarly, a forty-person party in Grand Canyon may seem big, but an approaching group of twenty or more bright orange inflatable kayaks on the Rogue River feels like an invading horde. The impact of other hunters is also greater when they fire too soon and drive the geese away or engage in inappropriate behaviors such as disturbing game or littering. These complicating factors are important but hard to predict and control, and in this book we have made the simplifying assumption that all types of encounters have roughly the same impact. Further research should begin to take these differences into account.

The remainder of Appendix 1 lists specific questionnaire items used to measure carrying capacity variables. They are included here as a reference for those designing capacity studies.

Reported Contacts

*During your trip, about how many times each day did you *actually* see another river party? If you saw the same party more than once, count each occasion separately.

We actually saw other parties about _____ times per day.

During your trip, about how many times each day did you see another river party? If you saw the same party more than once, count each occasion separately (circle one).

Day 1:	0	1-3	4-6	7-9	10-15	16-20	21-30	Over 30
Day 2:	0	1-3	4-6	7-9	10-15	16-20	21-30	Over 30
Day 3:	0	1-3	4-6	7-9	10-15	16-20	21-30	Over 30
Day 4:	0	1-3	4-6	7-9	10-15	16-20	21-30	Over 30
Day 5:	0	1-3	4-6	7-9	10-15	16-20	21-30	Over 30

About how many canoes did you see?

_____ none   _____ 10 to 20
_____ less than 5   _____ 20 to 30
_____ 5 to 10   _____ more than 30

About how many fishermen did you see?

_____ none   _____ 10 to 20
_____ less than 5   _____ 20 to 30
_____ 5 to 10   _____ more than 30

Preferred measure

About how many hunters other than those in your own party did you see in the field?

_____ none   _____ 11 to 15
_____ 1 to 2   _____ 16 to 30
_____ 3 to 5   _____ 21 to 30
_____ 6 to 10   _____ More than 30

Satisfaction

Overall, how would you rate your trip?
_____ Poor
_____ Fair, it just didn't work out very well
_____ Good, but I wish a number of things could have been different
_____ Very good, but could have been better
_____ Excellent, only minor problems
_____ Perfect

Perceived Crowding
Single Item
*Did you feel the river was crowded?

1	2	3	4	5	6	7	8	9
Not at all		Slightly crowded			Moderately crowded			Extremely crowded

Preferred measure

Multiple Item Scale

Item	Extent
Our trip would have been better if we had fewer people along the way.	0.66
The places we stopped (like Redwall Canyon) were often too crowded.	0.60
It bothered me to see so many people at side stops.	0.75
I don't think we met too many people during our trip down the river.	0.56
Too often we had to share a place like Deer Creek Falls with other groups.	0.60
I would have enjoyed the trip more if we had seen less people at side stops.	0.79
It bothered me to meet so many people while floating on the river.	0.74
I would have enjoyed the trip more if there hadn't been so many boats going by.	0.77
I would have enjoyed the trip more if we had seen less people while floating on the river.	0.88

Reliability = 0.91, mean = 18.6, S.D. = 6.6.

Expectations
*Before you went on this trip, about how many times each day did you *expect* to see other parties?

I expected to see other parties _____ times per day

_____ I didn't know what to expect

Did you expect to see more _____, about the same _____, or fewer parties _____?

Preferences
*How many times each day would you *prefer* to see other parties?

_____ times per day.

Would you prefer to see more _____, about the same _____, or fewer _____ other parties?

Preferred measure

Contact Norms (Grand Canyon Public Involvement Meetings)

Different people have different ideas about river trips in Grand Canyon. We are asking you to think of the "Grand Canyon experience" in three different ways. You can then indicate which one you think is most appropriate.

I. Imagine the Canyon as a "wilderness," a place generally unaffected by the presence of man. If the canyon were this kind of area, which of the following encounter levels would be appropriate? Indicate the *highest* level you would tolerate before the trip would no longer be a "wilderness experience."

Number of encounters with other parties while floating on the river each day.

OK to have as many as _____ encounters per day.

_____ makes no difference to me.

Number of nights spent camping within sight of another party.

OK to be near others as many as _____ out of 10 nights.

_____ makes no difference to me.

II. Now imagine the Grand Canyon as a "semiwilderness," the kind of place where complete solitude is not expected. In this case, which encounter levels would be appropriate? Indicate the *highest* level you would tolerate before the trip would no longer be a "semiwilderness" experience.

OK to have as many as _____ encounters per day.

_____ makes no difference to me.

Number of nights spent camping within sight of another party.

OK to be near others as many as _____ out of 10 nights.

_____ makes no difference to me.

III. Now imagine the Grand Canyon as an "undeveloped recreation area," the kind of place where a natural setting is provided but meeting other people is part of the experience. In this case, which encounter levels would be appropriate? Indicate the point at which there would be too many people for even this kind of "undeveloped recreation" experience.

OK to have as many as _____ encounters per day.

_____ makes no difference to me.

Number of nights spent camping within sight of another party.

OK to be near others as many as _____ out of 10 nights.

_____ makes no difference to me.

Of the three kinds of experiences described above, which do you think the river trip in Grand Canyon *currently provides* (circle one).

       wilderness   semiwilderness   undeveloped recreation

Of the three kinds of experiences described above, which do you think the river trip in Grand Canyon *should provide* (circle one).

       wilderness   semiwilderness   undeveloped recreation

If you prefer "wilderness," would you be willing to do any of the following things in order to accomplish this? (circle one answer for each item)

Pay $100 more for the trip	No	Yes
Wait a year longer to go on the trip	No	Yes
Take the trip during the winter season (October through March)	No	Yes

Contact Norms (Brule River Questionnaire)

In this next section we need to ask a number of very similar questions to get an idea of how you react to seeing other visitors.

Do you find it a pleasant or an unpleasant experience? Or does it make no difference? We hate to ask you so many similar questions, but to compare our results with other surveys, it is necessary.

The questions are divided into three sections. The first section refers to fishermen, the second to canoers, and the last section refers to tubers.

Please answer all three sections. A party would include from 1 or 2 up to 5 people.

VU = Very unpleasant
u = Unpleasant
N = Neutral (do not care either way)
p = Pleasant
VP = Very pleasant

Section I.

1. What would be your feelings about seeing no other parties each day, neither fishermen, canoers nor tubers? VU u N p VP
2. What would be your feelings toward seeing 1 fisherman each day? VU u N p VP
3. Toward seeing 2 fishermen each day? VU u N p VP
4. Toward seeing 3 fishermen each day? VU u N p VP
5. Toward seeing 5 fishermen each day? VU u N p VP
6. Toward seeing 7 fishermen each day? VU u N p VP
7. Toward seeing 9 fishermen each day? VU u N p VP
8. Toward seeing 15 fishermen each day? VU u N p VP
9. Toward seeing 20 fishermen each day? VU u N p VP
10. Toward seeing 25 fishermen each day? VU u N p VP

(Identical sections for canoers and tubers)

Appendix 2
Setting Up Carrying Capacity Studies

Carrying capacity studies begin with a look at the broad picture. What is the area like and what do people do there? Are there over-use problems? If so, where are they concentrated? What are the political or resource limitations that govern potential remedies? This appendix outlines the background information which will help determine the need for a carrying capacity study. This review results in a decision to either drop the issue, manage the situation on the basis of existing information, or proceed with more formal research on ecological, physical, facility, or social capacity.

Background Information

Background information should describe (1) the context in which the resource is found, (2) the resource itself, and (3) the recreational activities occurring within the area. Information categories are summarized in the outline presented in Table A2-1; the text elaborates and provides examples.

General Context

The site to be studied occurs in geographical and political context. The *geographic context* is physical and observable. What is the surrounding area like? What are the major population centers? What about access to the resource? How is the resource connected with surrounding areas in terms of economic activity?

The Colorado River in Grand Canyon, for example, is fairly isolated. The canyon walls have for years been a barrier to people trying to cross the area, and the rapids prevented extensive river travel until just recently. The desert's lack of water has further limited development. The result is a 225-mile stretch of river with several trails, a few buildings, and no roads. Population centers are not close, and visitors usually travel great distances to reach the area. River running activity is relatively new and the river as a whitewater resource has relatively little impact on local communities.

The geographic context of the Rogue River provides a contrast. The river valley is a corridor through the Siskiyou Mountains, and roads and developments have been concentrated along its banks. Although the wild section of the river is less developed than other parts, it still has three road access points within the 40-mile stretch that we studied. Because the river itself has been used for travel, there are private homes and lodges scattered along the water's edge.

Political climates are more complex, although they are often related to geography. In resource management, political factors usually revolve around interest groups and managing agencies. Interest groups range from well-organized and outspoken factions to scattered individuals who are less likely to be heard. The former category includes conservation organizations, activity groups, key contact persons, landowners, concessioners, interested legislators, and so on. It is important to identify different interests, summarize their positions, understand differences among them, and assess their relative political influence.

Agencies are the other part of the political picture. There may be only one agency involved, as there was in Grand Canyon, or there may be several with overlapping jurisdictions. There were six agencies involved with managing the Rogue: the U.S. Forest Service and Bureau of Land Management, which controlled the land on both sides of the river; the Oregon State Marine Board, which was responsible for establishing regulation; the Oregon State Scenic Waterways Program, in which the Rogue was included; and the Josephine and Curry County Sheriff's Departments, which were responsible for enforcement.

Different agencies are likely to have different mandates and goals, both legal and philosophical. An obvious contrast is that between the Forest Service, which has a multiple use mandate and extensive experience with consumptive uses, and the Park Service, whose mandate for preservation and enjoyment is tied primarily to appreciative recreational uses. There may also be federal, state, or local legislation affecting the resource and its use, and budgetary and personnel constraints are always an issue.

The Resource Itself

A *physical description* of the resource is important in understanding the area and its problems. This includes terrain, land ownership, entry and exit points, and focal points such as camps, attraction sites, parking areas, or other facilities. Physical developments such as buildings, ramps, and transportation systems need to be included, as do visitor services such as concessions, rentals, guide services, and stores.

The physical description should not overlook unique factors affecting the resource. Glen Canyon Dam, for example, has a tremendous effect on float use in Grand Canyon. "Normal" water flows fluctuate from 5,000 to 30,000 cubic feet per second, depending on power demands in urban areas

Table A2-1. Background information for capacity studies.

A. *General Context in Which Resource Exists*
  1. *Geographical context*
      a. Nature of surrounding area
      b. Population centers
      c. Access (roads, air routes, etc.)
  2. *Political climate*
      a. Identify interest groups (activity clubs, conservation organizations, key contacts, landowners, concessions, businesses, influential individuals, interested individuals, interested legislators, etc.)
      b. Specify positions of interested groups (briefly summarize each)
      c. What agencies are involved?
          Jurisdictions of agencies
          Agency goals and mandates (legal, philosophical)
          Applicable legislation (federal, state, local)

B. *Factors Specific to the Resource*
  1. *Physical description*
      a. Terrain
      b. Entry and exit points
      c. Location of focal points, areas of use concentration (camps, attraction sites, put-in and take-out points, parking areas, facilities such as stores)
      d. Land ownership (public *vs.* private, groups and organizations, etc.)
      e. Major factors affecting resource use (e.g. dams, water rights, etc.)
      f. Developments and visitor services (buildings, ramps, roads, transportation systems, concessions, outfitters, stores, etc.)
  2. *Management*
      a. Who are the managers?
          Positions, titles
          Personalities, length of service, flexibility
          Who makes what decisions
          Formal chain of command
          Informal chain of command
      b. Management objectives for the resource
          General
          Restate in specific operational terms—what do you want to provide?
          Are objectives flexible?
  3. *User description*
      a. Where do visitors come from and how do they arrive?
      b. Demographic characteristics (age, income, group composition)
      c. Organizational aspects (clubs, organized activities, etc.)
  4. *Past and present use levels*
      a. People per year and changes and trends over past few years
      b. Identify problems in general and by area, group, type of use.

C. *Recreational Activities*
  1. *What do people do?*
     a. Name and describe activities
     b. Travel modes
     c. Travel patterns
        Space (Where do they go?)
        Time (How long does it take? Day use, overnight, extended use)
  2. *Detailed description of activity*
     a. Ideal
     b. As currently available
     c. Minimal requirements
     d. Differences in *a-c* above for different groups (e.g. beginners *vs.* advanced)
     e. Descriptions in *a-c* need to cover at least space necessary, facilities necessary, desirable ecological characteristics of environment, and "quality" experience in relation to numbers of people.
  3. *Which activities are considered "legitimate,"* which are not? (Value premises—may be legal or informal)
  4. *Which activities conflict with one another?*
  5. *Are there differences of opinion* about whether things are O.K.? For which activities?

D. *Substitute Activities*
  1. *Nature of substitutes*
  2. *Specific activities*
  3. *Availability of substitutes*
  4. *Differences in substitutability* by activity type and user group

E. *Rough Estimates of Capabilities* (specify assumptions regarding technology and norms under each category)
  1. *Ecological*
  2. *Physical*
  3. *Facilities*
  4. *Social*
  5. *Decide which type* of capacity is most likely to:
     a. Be the limiting factor
     b. Require the most information and work

F. *Anticipate Implementation Procedure and Possible Impacts*
  1. *Implementation*
     a. *What* will limits be?
     b. *Where* will they be applied?
     c. *How* will they be enforced, complied with, etc?
  2. *Kinds of impacts*
     a. Economic—how will resources be distributed?
     b. Social—how will experience change?
     c. Resource—how will area change physically?
  3. *Who will be impacted*
     a. All interest groups
     b. "Silent" folks
     c. Users (different impacts for different groups?)

as far away as Phoenix and Los Angeles. This changes water levels 5-10 vertical feet in some parts of the canyon. This means that some schemes to spread out departure times would be unsuccessful because the water level is not high enough to run the first rapid until late morning.

Knowledge about *management* is important in understanding an area. The idea is to go beyond simply naming the agency. A list of relevant positions and titles is helpful, but it is important to know who makes what decisions. Is the formal chain of command different from the informal one? What about the people occupying management positions? Have they been around long enough to know what is going on and be respected within the agency and the community? Are the decision makers flexible and open to new information, or entrenched in a certain way of looking at things? Will researchers have strong allies if problems arise, or will people quietly step aside when someone turns on the political heat? The answers to these questions are important to the study design and implementation.

The Bureau of Land Management, for example, had a specific Rogue River Area Manager, and ideally he would have been our primary contact during the study. It turned out, however, that people both above and below were working around him, so getting things done required that we follow suit. The overlapping jurisdictions mentioned earlier meant that a number of other personalities were involved, some receptive to new information and some not. The State Marine Board, for example, was made up of five political appointees with diverse points of view; some supported the Bureau of Land Mangagement's attempts to regulate river use, while others appeared to oppose virtually everything on principle. Working with managers was like working with several teams of horses pulling in different directions.

The Grand Canyon was simpler because there was only one agency, but we still learned a few lessons the hard way. When the research was planned, we talked to the Associate Regional Director as well as the park's Superintendent, Chief of Resource Management and others. All agreed about issues and data needs and indicated a willingness to allow experimentation in the research design. It later turned out, however, that manipulation of river travel required cooperation from the Inner Canyon Manager. It was his basic position that a reasonable capacity had already been established (based on the ranger's work load at Lee's Ferry) and that any substantial change of schedules was too disruptive. His superiors were reluctant to override his decisions, and his will generally prevailed. Better understanding of his role and more direct contact early in the study would have helped.

Objectives for the resource provide additional information about management. Often there are none, or they may be so general that they do not offer much guidance. A common objective is to "provide high-quality recreation opportunities" in the particular setting. This is a nice idea that few would question, but it is too vague to be much help in establishing policies. High-quality recreation ranges from remote backcountry experiences to

Disneyland; obviously no one purports to cover this spectrum in one area, so objectives need to be more specific. A more clear objective might be to "provide a wilderness backpacking experience," which could be further refined with operational statements such as "limit encounters among parties to three to five per day" or "provide opportunities to camp out of sight and sound of others all of the time."

Developing and clarifying objectives is hard work, but the payoff is usually worth the effort. It is often an ongoing process into which new information is incorporated as it becomes available. In Grand Canyon, for example, most of the inner canyon had traditionally been managed as wilderness and an early study showed that most people thought of the area in this way. Over a period of several years this crystallized as a management objective, and a 1975 master plan said that the Park Service intended to provide a wilderness experience on trips through the canyon. But there was still controversy over whether motorized trips fit with this objective. Data from the sociological study showed that rowing trips were longer, involved fewer people, used smaller boats with less people per boat, and stopped at more off-river attraction sites (Shelby and Nielsen 1976a). Passengers on an experimental combination trip reported that oar trips traveled at a more relaxed pace, that social groupings were more comfortable, and that it was easier to get interpretive information from boatmen. Seeing these data, park managers further defined the "wilderness river experience" objective in terms of a leisurely pace, opportunities for social interaction and interpretation, and provision for off-river side trips. These objectives, combined with the data describing trip differences, supported a decision to phase out motors in the canyon (see Shelby 1980 for further information). The point is that the objectives were somewhat flexible, and they became more clear over time as we learned about the different recreation experiences.

The *users themselves* are another factor specific to the resource. Where do they come from and how do they arrive? Is there any information about their demographic characteristics, either from previous studies or casual observation? Are users organized by clubs or other activity-oriented groups?

The Grand Canyon is internationally known as a scenic wonder, and river travelers come from all over the country, many arriving by air. The surrounding area is sparsely populated, so there is not much local use. In contrast, Rogue River users are more regional. They come primarily from the population centers in Oregon's Willamette Valley and Northern California. There is also a large local contingent from the cities of Grants Pass and Medford, which are located in the Rogue River Valley. Goose hunters at Grand River Marsh are even more local; most are from southeastern Wisconsin, less than two hours' drive from the area.

Most areas with carrying capacity problems have some records of *past and present use levels*. The quality of such data varies greatly, so it is a good idea to inquire about sources and interpret the figures cautiously. Managers at

Grand Canyon had fairly accurate records of use going back to John Wesley Powell's first trip in 1879, which showed there had been little use before 1960, but that activity had increased almost 60 percent per year after Lake Powell was filled in 1966. In contrast, Department of Natural Resource managers on the Brule River had data for only the past three to four years, the quality of which was doubtful. An electric eye counter had been installed and was supposed to be read weekly; but sometimes the reading was not done, sometimes the device was broken, and sometimes people who found the counter moved back and forth in front of it to run up the count. Grand River Marsh is an example where data on use levels were simply nonexistent. The DNR had occasionally sent people to check hunter success rates, but they did not count the cars in the parking lot or the number of hunters while they were there counting ducks and geese.

Use patterns may vary by user group, type of use, or by area within the resource. In Grand Canyon, for example, the tremendous growth in the late 1960s and early 1970s was primarily due to increases in commercial use by outfitters. After limitations went into effect in 1973, the number of applications for private do-it-yourself permits increased dramatically. On the Rogue, recent increases have been primarily in float use, while jet boat use has remained more nearly constant. Use problems also tend to be concentrated in time and space; all the deer hunters go out once a year on opening day, and the firing line goose hunters all stand in a row along the edge of the marsh.

Recreational Activities

What do people do in the area? The idea is to name and then describe the activities in detail. How do people travel? What are the travel routes and destinations, and how long does it take to get from one place to another? Do people stay for two to three weeks, as some do in Grand Canyon, or only a few hours, like the goose hunters? Are some activities more "legitimate" than others, and are there conflicts among activities and differences of opinion about the situation?

It is usually helpful to think of each activity as it would occur under ideal circumstances, as it is currently available, and in terms of minimal requirements. Differences between these three levels will highlight problems or potential problems and suggest the experience parameters on which evaluative standards are based. These descriptions should include information about desirable *ecological* characteristics, necessary *physical* space, required facilities, and appropriate amounts of *contact* with other users. The information can be obtained from managers, observation, and/or conversations with a few users. It is not intended to take the place of more comprehensive measurements of experience parameters and evaluative standards, but rather to provide an initial understanding of activities and help determine the dimensions which need measuring. Keep in mind that activity requirements may be different for different groups (e.g. beginners or more advanced participants).

An example from the Brule River may help to illustrate. Trout anglers along the Brule arrive earlier than other recreationists. Many begin fishing at dawn, almost all before 10:00 a.m. Some start at Stones Bridge and canoe downstream to Winneboujou Bridge, while others park near one of the bridges or other places where the road is close to the river and wade up- or downstream. Almost all are done fishing by midafternoon, although some return in the early evening.

Anglers travel at a slow pace. They stop in deep spots and slow sections to fish the quiet holes, and those in canoes may even get out to wade back along the bank. They may fish a good spot for ten to thirty minutes. Fishers in a canoe need more space than recreational paddlers because fishing lines extend out from the canoe. Wading anglers occupy a similarly large space. Anglers also look ahead to the next good fishing hole; someone disturbing that spot may also encroach on their activity.

Ideally, then, anglers would like to have a fairly large amount of physical space. The ecosystem requirements for good trout habitat (clear, cold water, minimal algae growth, etc.) are essential to the activity, as are aesthetic qualities which differentiate trout fishing on the Brule from, for example, still fishing in a reservoir. Anglers also prefer to see few other people, partly so others will not actually interfere, but also because trout fishing is viewed as a somewhat solitary activity. Facility requirements are minimal; all fishers need is a place to park and a rough footpath to the river.

The fishing experience actually available on the Brule at the time of our study was somewhat less than ideal, at least during the middle of the day. Facilities and ecological characteristics were not a problem, but anglers complained about interference from tubers and recreational canoers. They also felt that the only time they could have a solitary fishing experience was early in the morning. Minimal requirements for most fishers meant lack of interference; seeing a few other people was undesirable but did not necessarily ruin the experience.

As this example suggests, there may be several activities taking place on the same resource. If there are, what are the conflicts? Are some activities considered more "legitimate" (either by users or managers) than others? What are the value premises which make some things more appropriate than others? The values may be legal (e.g., "motorized vehicles are prohibited in this area") or less formal (hikers or paddlers just do not like trail bikes or motorboats). Do the groups view each other differently? Oar travelers in Grand Canyon, for example, were more bothered by motorized use than motor travelers were by oar trips. There may also be differences of opinion about the acceptability of the current situation. Anglers on the Brule, for example, were bothered by the recent influx of canoers and tubers, but the tubers seemed quite satisfied.

Substitute Activities

The extensive information gathered on primary activities can be supplemented by information about the alternatives available to users. What areas besides the primary one offer the same activities? How far away are they? Are there different activities which users are willing to substitute? What are they, and how are they similar? Are some activities more easily substituted than others? Are some user groups more flexible?

The Brule River study provides an example. The questionnaire listed twenty-three other rivers and asked respondents which ones they had used for their activity. Participants also rated the desirability of these rivers in comparison to the Brule. Results suggested that most people had used other rivers, but none of these were considered better. Anglers and canoers had more alternatives available, but these activities also had the longest tradition on the Brule. Tubers had fewer substitutes but showed less overall commitment to their activity. This analysis of substitutes helped assess the implications of banning any particular group.

At Grand Canyon, data on substitutes were not gathered, although in retrospect we believe this would have been helpful. Some have argued that commercial passengers might be just as happy with something like a trip to Hawaii, while others claim that private river runners just run other rivers when they cannot get a Grand Canyon permit. It is possible that private users are more likely to substitute another (though probably less desirable) river, while commercial passengers are more likely to substitute a different activity altogether. This kind of information is extremely helpful in weighing the consequences of different policies. If another easily accessible area offers the same activity, little is lost and people are likely to make the shift fairly cheerfully. Greater care is required when no substitutes are available.

Rough Estimates of Capacities

With background information in hand, it is time to start thinking about research. Before actually collecting any data, it is helpful to make rough estimates for each of the four types of carrying capacity (ecological, physical, facility, social). This procedure will help specify assumptions about the relevant management, and impact parameters and evaluative standards. It will also suggest which type of capacity is likely to be the limiting factor, and therefore which is likely to require more information and further work.

For Brule River fishers, the *physical* capacity would be the number of fishers that could actually fish on the river. Calculating the size of a canoe as the boat itself plus a 2-yard extension in all directions and the size of wading fisher as a circle with a 20-yard radius, we could determine approximately how many fishers will fit in the available water. Note the assumption about space requirements which allows a fisher to cast in any direction. If casting were restricted to only one direction, anglers could be packed shoulder to shoulder, resulting in a much higher physical capacity.

Facility capacity in this case does not appear to be a problem. Parking areas are the only major facilities, and these are expanded at high-use times by parking along the shoulders or roadways. Bathroom facilities are another consideration, but these are unlikely to impose limits because there is little overnight use and bushes are abundant. Facility capacity, then, is likely to be quite high. This judgment assumes present parking techniques. If local law enforcement officials started ticketing cars parked along shoulders, facility capacity would go down.

Ecological capacity is another consideration. Trout fishing does little to pollute the water, raise water temperature, or otherwise disturb fish habitat. As long as fishers do not throw trash, floating on the river does not have easily observable effects, although wading in gravel beds may disturb spawning. Fishing pressure, then, is the major factor affecting ecological capacity. The assumption here is a natural fish habitat and a sustained yield of fish; stocking or feeding fish could greatly increase the allowable harvest while maintaining a constant fish population over time. Streamside trampling and trailing might be another consideration.

Social capacity depends on what fishers consider appropriate encounter levels. Trout fishing is ideally a solitary sport. Anglers seem to tolerate a few encounters, but they also need more space than the physical minimum to cast their lines. Social capacity, then, seems to be the major issue.

Implementation and Impacts

Implementation should be considered before research begins; a well thought out capacity can be destroyed if it is put into practice badly. What will the limits be? Where will they be applied? Is compliance as convenient for users as monitoring and enforcement are for managers? Obviously, it will not be possible to provide definitive answers at this stage, but the exercise suggests data needs and points out potential pitfalls.

Enforcement of use limits in Grand Canyon is relatively easy because the Park Service has a full-time ranger at Lee's Ferry and users have been complying with interim regulations since 1973. In contrast, regulation on the Brule would be considerably more difficult. Users are not accustomed to being regulated, and there are numerous access points along the river.

What other impacts will a capacity plan have? Will there be economic effects as a result of shifting dollars or resources from one area to another? What will be the social impacts on the experience (as a result of limits, routing, scheduling, etc.)? Will there be changes in the natural resource or the facilities provided? Which interest groups will be affected, and what about users and others who are less vocal? The idea is to determine major impacts which preclude certain alternatives as well as to think about more subtle impacts which may hamper the implementation process.

Consider the management plan proposed for Grand Canyon. One policy is to allow more use by private trips. If this were done by subtracting user days from the commercial sector, a very vocal and politically powerful interest group would be affected economically. The plan avoided formal on-river scheduling of camps or stops because this impact on the experience was seen as undesirable. Some have argued that use limitation will raise the price of commercial trips, making them unavailable to those with lower incomes (a group not often represented in the decision process). Simple economic theory suggests that prices will rise as long as demand increases and use is limited, but data show that river runners are generally a well-to-do group, and the expense involved in taking time off from work and traveling to and from the area often outweighs the price of the river trip itself.

Social Capacity Studies

The process described above results in a substantial amount of information about the resource, recreational activities, and the kinds of limits which are likely to be most important. The problem now is to determine the need for a formal capacity study. If ecological, physical, or facility capacity appeared most likely to be the limiting factor, more extensive study in one of those areas may be in order. The general model developed in Chapter 1 can be used to design such studies, although our focus is on social capacity studies. It has been our experience, however, that social capacity is often the most critical in the long run. Ecological impacts can often be mitigated by management parameters other than use level, physical capacity is usually quite high, and facilities can be expanded or made more efficient.

There may already be enough information to specify a social capacity. This can be determined by going back to the rough social capacity estimate and seeing how well the conditions specified by the three rules have been satisfied. Capacity can be set if there is (1) a known relationship between management and experience parameters; (2) agreement among relevant groups about the type of experience to be provided; and (3) agreement among relevant groups about the appropriate level of the experience parameters.

There are two sets of circumstances under which a social capacity study will not be necessary. First, it is possible that the review of available information will satisfy the three rules. For example, managers might know from patrol trips and other observations that high use results in competition for campsites, and they may be able to make a reasonably accurate guess about some lower level which would eliminate the problem. The review might also show general agreement about the kind of experience to be provided and the relevant evaluative standard (e.g., no competition for camps). In this case it would be possible to determine and implement a capacity without further study, particularly if the political environment would allow some lack of precision. This, of course, is most likely to be found early in the game, before increased use levels have created major problems and controversy.

A study may also be unnecessary if the review shows lack of agreement about the experience to be provided. In Wisconsin, for example, there are two alternative views of the deer hunting experience. Some hunters prefer to be alone, while others like to see other hunters. If background information suggests strong disagreement about what should be provided, it may be difficult to determine a single capacity. If recreationists have sufficient opportunity to select high- or low-density settings, a single capacity may be unnecessary. As long as recreational use continues to increase, however, the failure to make capacity determinations is a *de facto* decision to move away from low-density recreation and provide opportunities for experiences involving higher numbers of people.

Appendix 3
Data Describing Allocation Systems

A use-history based on permit data is a great help in setting up and evaluating allocation systems. Data should be analyzed each year at the end of the season. When necessary, other information about user characteristics and preferences can be collected by sampling the user population defined by the permits. This requires a special research effort.

Data Collection

Initial Contact

Data collection begins when a user contacts the agency for a permit. The agency records the application date, how the application is made (mail, personal visit, telephone, etc.) and the expected trip description (who will go and length of trip). This forms the baseline from which later calculations are made. Information is organized most simply by assigning each permit request a unique identification number to which information gathered at later times can be added.

Between Initial Contact and Participation

Requests can be treated in one of three ways: (1) a permit is issued as requested; (2) a permit is issued with modifications (e.g., rescheduling the date or location); or (3) the permit is denied. If a permit is issued, any modifications are noted. If the permit is denied, the reason for denial is recorded and data collection for that application ends. If there is a cancellation any time before the start of the trip, the cancellation is recorded and data collection ends.

Day of Arrival

If a permittee fails to show up, this information is recorded and data collection ends. If the permittee arrives as scheduled, data describing the trip can be collected. These include: the final trip roster, length of trip, mode of travel, and type of trip. The entire data collection process is summarized in Table A3-1.

Table A3-1. Summary of data collection procedure.

Initial Contact
1. Give each request unique ID number.
2. Record how the request is made (personal visit, telephone, mail, etc.)
3. Record date application was received.
4. Record requested launch date.
5. Record expected trip length.
6. Record expected trip roster (names).

Between Contact and Launch

Is permit rejected?   *yes*—Record reason, stop recording
  no

Is permit modified?   *yes*—Record modification
  no

Record permit issue date

Did the group cancel before launch?   *no*—Go to launch day
  yes

Record cancellation date, stop recording

Launch Day

Did the group show up?   *no*—Record as "no-show," stop recording
  yes
1. Record date of launch.
2. Record type and number of craft (raft, kayak, drift boat, etc.).
3. Record length of trip.
4. Compare actual roster with original and record number of passengers requested, final number taken, and percentage of names changed.

Data Analysis

Most agencies collect use data, but the information is often left in a raw form which is not useful. Data analysis means deciding what aggregate figures are desired and then compiling the information from the raw data. Some of the more useful computations would include:

(1) The number of applications received each day from different kinds of users (e.g., private and commercial users), tallied on a calendar. This would show planning horizons.

(2) The number of permits requested for each day aggregated by day of the week, month of the season, and total for the season. This would show use patterns, peak use periods, and yearly changes for different user groups.

(3) Percentage of applications which are issued, rescheduled,and rejected, and the reasons for rescheduling or rejecting.

(4) Percentage of cancellations and no-shows (by user group, method of making reservation, and length of lead time).

(5) Number of trips and people, aggregated by day of the week, by month, and by season. When compared with (2), this would show how actual use patterns compare with requests.

(6) The average number of days in advance of the start of the trip that permits are requested, separated by user group. This will give information about lead times.

(7) Percentage of names changed from initial to final roster, and average increase or decrease in group size.

System Costs

The costs of the permit system should be separated from other management expenditures and divided into nonrecurring development and recurring operating costs. Combining the two will give the total cost of administering the system. Cost data will be useful in determining the cost-effectiveness of different alternatives. Cost data should include:

Development costs
wages and salaries
planning
equipment and hardware
computer programming
uniforms
training
facility construction or
modification

Operating costs
wages and salaries
expendable materials
management and supervision
utilities (e.g., telephone)
facility maintenance

Bibliography

Alaska, State of. 1977. *Special Hunt Seasons and Regulations*. Alaska Department of Fish and Game. Pamphlet.

Alldredge, R.B. 1973. Some capacity theory for parks and recreation areas. *Trends* October/December:20-30.

Altman, I. 1975. *The Environment and Social Behavior*. Monterey: Brooks/Cole Publishing Co.

Anderson, F.J., and N.C. Bonsor. 1974. Allocation, congestion, and the valuation of recreational resources. *Land Economics* 50(Feb):51-57.

Anonymous. 1974. Computer magic: Hotel presses button, labor waste vanishes. *Institutions and Volume Feeding*, May.

Arizona, State of. 1977. *Hunting Regulations, 1977-1978*. Arizona Department of Fish and Game. Pamphlet.

Badger, T.J. 1975. Rawah Wilderness crowding tolerances and some management techniques: An aspect of social carrying capacity. M.S. Thesis. Colorado State University, Ft. Collins. 83 pp.

Baldassare, M. 1978. *Residential Crowding in Urban America*. Berkeley: University of California Press.

Becker, R.H., A. Jubenville, and G.W. Burnett. 1984. Fact and judgment in the search for a social carrying capacity. *Leisure Sciences* 6(4):475-486.

Becker, R.H., B.J. Niemann, and W.A. Gates. 1979. Displacement of users within a river system: Social and environmental tradeoffs. Paper presented at the American Institute of Biological Sciences' Second Conference on Scientific Research in the National Parks, November 27-31, 1979. San Francisco.

Bishop, R.C., and T.A. Heberlein. 1979. Measuring values of extramarket goods: Are indirect measures biased? *American Journal of Agricultural Economics* 61(5):926-930.

Bratton, S.P., M.G. Hickler, and J.H. Graves. 1977. *Trail and Campground Erosion Survey for Great Smoky Mountains National Park*. USDI National Park Service Management Report No. 16. Washington, D.C.

Braybooke, D., and C.E. Lindblom. 1963. *A Strategy of Decision*. New York: Free Press.

Brown, P.J. 1977. Whitewater rivers: Social inputs to carrying capacity based decisions. Pages 97-122 in *Managing Colorado River Whitewater—The Carrying Capacity Strategy*. Logan: Utah State University Department of Forestry and Outdoor Recreation.

Buist, L.J. 1981. *Recreation Use Allocation*. Number R-149. Reno, Nevada: Nevada Agricultural Experiment Station.

Bultena, G.L., D. Field, P. Womble, and D. Albrecht. 1981. Closing the gates: A study of backcountry use-limitation at Mount McKinley National Park. *Leisure Sciences* 4(3):249-267.

Burch, W.R., Jr. 1981. The ecology of metaphors—spacing regularities for humans and other primates in urban and wildland habitats. *Leisure Sciences* 4(3):213-230.

Burch, W.R., Jr. 1984. Much ado about nothing—some reflections on the wider and wilder implications of social carrying capacity. *Leisure Sciences* 6(4):487-496.

Burnett, James T. III. 1973. Campground reservation systems. . . A study. *Trends*, April-June.

Bury, R.L. 1976. Recreational carrying capacity. *Parks and Recreation* 11(1):22-25, 56-57.

Butler, E.A., and D.M. Knudson. 1977. *Recreational Carrying Capacity*. Indiana Outdoor Recreation Planning Program 1975-79, Element No. 16.

Cahn, R. 1968. Will success spoil the National Parks? *The Christian Science Monitor*. Boston, Massachusetts: The Christian Science Publishing Society. 55 pp.

Campbell, A., P.E. Converse, and W.L. Rogers. 1976. *The Quality of American Life: Perceptions, Evaluations, and Satisfactions*. New York: Russell Sage Foundation.

Cancian, F.M. 1975. *What are Norms?* New York: Cambridge University Press.

Caughley, G. 1976. Wildlife management and the dynamics of ungulate populations. Pages 183-246 in T.H. Coaker (ed.), *Applied Biology*, Vol. 1. London: Academic Press.

Cicchetti, C.J., and V.K. Smith. 1973. Congestion, quality deterioration, and optimal use: Wilderness recreation in the Spanish Peaks Primitive Area. *Social Science Research* 2(1):15-30.

Cicchetti, C.J., and V.K. Smith. 1976. *The Costs of Congestion*. Cambridge, Massachusetts: Ballinger.

Clapsaddle, C., and J.C. Greenley. 1979. *Handling of Special Hunt Applications*. Idaho Department of Fish and Game. Mimeo.

Clark, R.N., and G.H. Stankey. 1979. *The Recreation Opportunity Spectrum: A Framework for Planning, Management, and Research*. USDA Forest Service General Technical Report PNW-98. Portland, Oregon: Pacific Northwest Forest and Range Experiment Station.

Clawson, M., and J.L. Knetsch. 1966. *Economics of Outdoor Recreation*. Baltimore: Johns Hopkins Press.

Cole, D.N. 1982. *Wilderness Campsite Impacts: Effect of Amount of Use*. USDA Forest Service Research Paper INT-284. Ogden, Utah: Intermountain Forest and Range Experiment Station. 34 pp.

Cole, D.N., and E.G. Schreiner. 1981. *Impacts of Backcountry Recreation: Site Management and Rehabilitation—An Annotated Bibliography*. USDA Forest Service General Technical Report INT-121. Ogden, Utah: Intermountain Forest and Range Experiment Station. 58 pp.

Conservation Foundation. 1972. *National Parks at the Crossroads—Drawing the Line Where Protection Ends and Overuse Begins.* Washington, D.C.: Conservation Foundation. 12 pp.

Cox, G.B. 1977. Managerial style: Implications for the utilization of program evaluation information. *Evaluation Quarterly* 1(3):499-508.

Dasmann, R.F. 1964. *Wildlife Biology.* New York: John Wiley and Sons.

Dekker, E.A. 1976. *Private Use on the Colorado River in Grand Canyon and Canyonlands National Parks.* Interim Report, National Park Service, Denver Service Center.

Desor, J.A. 1972. Toward a psychological theory of crowding. *Journal of Personality and Social Psychology* 21(1):79-83.

Deutsch, M. 1975. Equity, equality, and need: What determines which value will be used as the basis of distributive justice? *Journal of Social Issues* 31(3):108-118.

Ditton, R.B. 1979. *The Buffalo National River Recreation Study: Year One.* Prepared for the USDI National Park Service. Sante Fe, New Mexico: Southwest Region Office of Natural Resources.

Ditton, R.B., A.J. Fedler, and A.R. Graefe. 1982. Factors contributing to perceptions of recreation crowding. *Leisure Sciences* 5(4):273-288.

Ditton, R.B., A.R. Graefe, and A.J. Fedler. 1979. Recreational satisfaction at Buffalo National River: Some measurement concerns. Pages 491-506 in *Proceedings* of the Second Conference on Scientific Research in the National Parks. San Francisco, California: USDI National Park Service.

Dorfman, P.W. 1979. Measurement and meaning of recreation satisfaction: A case study in camping. *Environment and Behavior* 11:483-510.

Draft River Management Plan. 1977. In *Final Environmental Statement—*Proposed Colorado River Management Plan, Grand Canyon National Park, Arizona. 1979. National Park Service, Department of the Interior.

Driver, B.L., and R.C. Knopf. 1977. Personality, outdoor recreation and expected consequences. *Environment and Behavior* (9):169-193.

Faro, J. 1974. *Guidelines for the McNail State Game Sanctuary Permit System.* State of Alaska, Department of Fish and Game. Mimeo.

Fisher, A.C., and J.V. Krutilla. 1972. Determination of optimal capacity of resource based facilities. *Natural Resources Journal* 12(3):417-444.

Freedman, J.L. 1975. *Crowding and Behavior.* San Francisco: W.H. Freeman.

Friesema, H.P., and P.J. Culhane. 1976. Social impacts, politics, and the environmental impact statement process. *Natural Resources Journal* 16(2):339-356.

Frissell, S.S., Jr., and D.P. Duncan. 1965. Campsite preference and deterioration in the Quetico-Superior Canoe Country. *Journal of Forestry* 63(4):256-260.

Frissell, S.S., Jr., and G.H. Stankey. 1972. Wilderness environmental quality: Search for social and ecological harmony. Paper presented at Annual Meeting, Society of American Foresters, October 4. Hot Springs, Arkansas.

Galle, O., W. Gove, and J. McPherson. 1972. Population density and pathology: What are the relations for man? *Science* 176(7):309-316.

Graefe, A.R., J.J. Vaske, and A.B. Dempster. 1983. Perceived environmental quality models for wilderness recreation. Paper presented at the Fifth Annual Southeastern Recreation Researchers' Conference, February 1983. Asheville, North Carolina.

Graefe, A.R., J.J. Vaske, and F.R. Kuss. 1984a. Social carrying capacity: An integration and synthesis of twenty years of research. *Leisure Sciences* 6(4):395-432.

Graefe, A.R., J.J. Vaske, and F.R. Kuss. 1984b. Resolved issues and remaining questions about social carrying capacity. *Leisure Sciences* 6(4):497-508.

Gramann, J.H. 1982. Toward a behavioral theory of crowding in outdoor recreation: An evaluation and synthesis of research. *Leisure Sciences* 5(2):109-126.

Gruneberg, M.M. 1979. *Understanding Job Satisfaction*. London:Macmillan.

Hammitt, W.E., C.D. McDonald, and F.P. Noe. 1982. *Use Level and Encounters: Important Antecedents of Perceived Crowding Among Non-specialized Recreationists*. USDI National Park Service Southeast Regional Office and USDA Forest Service Southeastern Forest Experiment Station. Research Note. 13 pp.

Hardin, G. 1969. The economics of wilderness. *Natural History* 78(6):20-27.

Hawkins, J.D., R.A. Raffman, and P. Osborne. 1978. Decision maker's judgments: The influence of role, evaluative criteria, and information access. *Evaluation Quarterly* 2(3):435-454.

Heberlein, T.A. 1977. Density, crowding and satisfaction: Sociological studies for determining carrying capacities. Pages 67-76 in *Proceedings: River Recreation Management and Research Symposium*. USDA Forest Service Technical Report NC-28. St. Paul, Minnesota: North Central Forest Experiment Station.

Heberlein, T.A., G.E. Alfano, and L.H. Ervin. In press. Using a social carrying capacity model to estimate the effects of massive development at the Apostle Islands National Lakeshore. *Leisure Sciences* 8(3).

Heberlein, T.A., and B. Laybourne. 1978. *The Wisconsin Deer Hunter: Social Characteristics, Attitudes and Preferences for Proposed Hunting Season Changes*. Center for Resource Policy Studies, School of Natural Resources, College of Agriculture and Life Sciences, Working Paper No. 10. University of Wisconsin, Madison.

Heberlein, T.A., and B. Shelby. 1977. Carrying capacity, values, and the satisfaction model. *Journal of Leisure Research* 9(2):142-148.

Heberlein, T.A., and J.J. Vaske. 1977. *Crowding and Visitor Conflict on the Bois Brule River*. Water Resources Center, Technical Report #OWRT A-066-WAS. University of Wisconsin, Madison.

Helgath, S.F. 1975. *Trail Deterioration in the Selway-Bitterroot Wilderness*. USDA Forest Service Research Note INT-193. Ogden, Utah: Intermountain Forest and Range Experiment Station.

Hendee, J.C. 1974. A multiple-satisfaction approach to game management. *Wildlife Society Bulletin* 2(3):104-113.

Hendee, J.C., W.R. Catton, L.D. Marlow, and C.F. Brockman. 1968. *Wilderness Users in the Pacific Northwest—Their Characteristics, Values and Management Preferences.* USDA Forest Service Research Paper PNW-61. Portland, Oregon: Pacific Northwest Forest and Range Experiment Station.

Hendee, J.C., R.N. Clark, and T.E. Dailey. 1977. *Fishing and Other Recreation Behavior at High-Mountain Lakes in Washington State.* USDA Forest Service Research Note PNW-304. Portland, Oregon: Pacific Northwest Forest and Range Experiment Station.

Hendee, J.C., G.H. Stankey, and R.C. Lucas. 1978. *Wilderness Management.* Washington, D.C.: USDA Forest Service Miscellaneous Publication No. 1365.

Hudson, M. Cited in *Final Environmental Statement—Proposed Colorado River Management Plan.* National Park Service, Department of the Interior. Grand Canyon National Park, Arizona. pp. IX-147.

Jacob, G.R., and R. Schreyer. 1980. Conflict in outdoor recreation: A theoretical perspective. *Journal of Leisure Research* 12(4):368-380.

Joyner, S. 1977. Personal communication. Registered guide and outfitter. Savoonga, Alaska.

Kilgore, B.M. 1978. Views on natural science and resource management in the Pacific Northwest. Keynote address at the Science/Resources Management Workshop. National Park Service, Pacific Northwest Region, Seattle.

Kuss, F.R., A.R. Graefe, and J.J. Vaske. 1984. *Recreation Impacts and Carrying Capacity: A Review and Synthesis of Ecological and Social Research.* University of Maryland, College Park.

Langer, E.J., and S. Saegert. 1977. Crowding and cognitive control. *Journal of Personality and Social Psychology* 35(3):175-182.

Lawrence, J.E.S. 1974. Science and sentiment: Overview of research on crowding and human behavior. *Psychological Bulletin* 8(10):712-720.

Lee, R.G. 1975. *The Management of Human Components in the Yosemite National Park Ecosystem.* Yosemite, California: The Yosemite Institute. 134 pp.

Leventhall, G.S. 1976. The distribution of rewards in groups and organizations. In L. Berkowitz (ed.), *Advances in Experimental Social Psychology.* New York: Academic Press.

Lime, D.W. 1976. Wilderness use and users: A summary of research. In *Proceedings of the 54th annual winter meeting, Allegheny Section, Society of American Foresters.* Dover, Delaware. 163 pp.

Lime, D.W. 1977. Research for river recreation planning and management. Pages 202-209 in *River Recreation Management and Research Symposium Proceedings.* USDA Forest Service General Technical Report NC-28. St. Paul, Minnesota: North Central Forest Experiment Station.

Lindblom, C.E., and D.K. Cohen. 1979. *Usable Knowledge.* New Haven: Yale University Press.

Lucas, R.C. 1964. Wilderness perception and use: The example of the Boundary Waters Canoe Area. *Natural Resources Journal* 3(3):394-411.

Lucas, R.C. 1980. *Use Patterns and Visitor Characteristics, Attitudes and Preferences in Nine Wilderness and Other Roadless Areas.* USDA Forest Service Research Paper INT-253. Ogden, Utah: Intermountain Forest and Range Experiment Station. 89 pp.

Lucas, R.C., and J.L. Oltman. 1971. Survey sampling wilderness visitors. *Journal of Leisure Research* 3(1):28-43.

Lucas, R.C., and G.H. Stankey. 1974. Social carrying capacity for backcountry recreation. Pages 14-23 in *Outdoor Recreation Research: Applying the Results.* USDA Forest Service General Technical Report NO-9. St. Paul, Minnesota: North Central Forest Experiment Station.

Magill, A.W. 1973. *An Overview of Campground Reservation Systems.* USDA Forest Service, Pacific Southwest Forest Experiment Station. Mimeo.

Magill, A.W. 1976. *Campsite Reservation Systems. . . The Camper's Viewpoint.* USDA Forest Service Research Paper PSW-121.

Manning, R.E., and C.P. Ciali. 1980. Recreation density and user satisfaction: A further exploration of the satisfaction model. *Journal of Leisure Research* 12(4):329-345.

March, I.G., and H.A. Simon. 1958. *Organizations.* New York: Wiley and Sons.

McConnell, K.E. 1976. Congestion and willingness to pay: A study of beach use. *Land Economics* 53(2):185-195.

McCool, S.F., and M. Petersen. 1982. *An Application of the Two Factor Theory of Satisfaction to Recreational Settings.* Report submitted to Forestry Sciences Laboratory, Intermountain Forest and Range Experiment Station, Missoula, Montana.

McLaughlin, W.J., E.E. Krumpe, W.E.J. Paradice, W.C. Salvi, and M.W. Weesner. 1982. *The Flathead River Study Final Report.* Prepared for the Flathead National Forest, Kalispell, Montana and Glacier National Park, West Glacier, Montana. 195 pp.

Meinecke, E.P. 1928. *The Effect of Excessive Tourist Travel on the California Redwood Parks.* California State Printing Office, Sacramento. 20 pp.

Merriam, L.C., Jr., and C.K. Smith. 1974. Visitor impact on newly developed campsites in the Boundary Waters Canoe Area. *Journal of Forestry* 72(10):620-630.

Miller, P. 1981. "Regulating the last slices of wilderness." *Adventure Travel.* Feb-Mar:86-89.

National Park Service. 1974. *The Campsite Reservation System, A Pilot Program in Six National Parks.* Washington, D.C.: National Park Service.

Nielsen, J.M., and R. Endo. 1977. Where have all the purists gone? An empirical examination of the displacement process hypothesis in wilderness recreation. *Western Sociological Review* 8:61-75.

Oregon, State of. 1977. *Controlled Hunt Seasons and Regulations.* Oregon Department of Fish and Wildlife. Pamphlet.

Outdoor Recreation Resource Review Commission. 1962. *Outdoor Recreation for America*. Washington, D.C.: U.S. Government Printing Office.

Pauly, M.V., and T.D. Willett. 1972. Two concepts of equity and their implications for public policy. *Social Science Quarterly* 53(1).

Pfister, R.E., and R. Frenkel. 1974. *Field Investigation of River Use Within the Wild River Area of the Rogue River, Oregon*. Interim Report to the Oregon State Marine Board. Salem. 112 pp.

Rappoport, A. 1975. Toward a redefinition of density. *Environment and Behavior* 7(2):133-158.

Rausch, R.A. 1977. Personal communication. Director, Division of Game, State of Alaska.

Ream, C.H. 1980. *Impacts of Backcountry Recreationists on Wildlife: An Annotated Bibliography*. USDA Forest Service General Technical Report INT-81. Ogden, Utah: Intermountain Forest and Range Station. 63 pp.

Rinehart, J. 1977. Personal correspondence. Licensing Director, Wyoming Wild Game and Fish Department.

Rossi, P.H., and S.R. Wright. 1977. Evaluation research: An assessment of theory, practice, and policies. *Evaluation Quarterly* 1(1):5-51.

Sandfort, W. 1977. Personal correspondence. Licensing section, Colorado Division of Wildlife.

Schmidt, D., and J. Keating. 1979. Human crowding and personal control: An integration of the research. *Psychological Bulletin* 36(4):680-700.

Schmitt, R.C. 1966. Density, health, and social disorganization. *Journal of American Institute of Planners* 32(1):38-40.

Schreyer, R. 1976. Sociological and political factors in carrying capacity decision making. Pages 228-258 in *Proceedings of the Third Resources Management Conference*. Ft. Worth, Texas: USDI National Park Service, Southwest Region.

Schreyer, R., and M.L. Nielson. 1978. *Westwater and Desolation Canyons: Whitewater River Recreation*. Logan, Utah: Institute for the Study of Outdoor Recreation and Tourism, Utah State University. 196 pp.

Schreyer, R., and J.W. Roggenbuck. 1978. The influence of experience expectations on crowding perceptions and social psychological carrying capacities. *Leisure Sciences* 1(4):373-394.

Shelby, B. 1976. Social psychological effects of crowding in wilderness: The case of river trips in the Grand Canyon. Unpublished Dissertation, University of Colorado.

Shelby, B. 1980. Contrasting recreational experiences: Motors and oars in the Grand Canyon. *Journal of Soil and Water Conservation* 35(3):129-131.

Shelby, B. 1981a. Encounter norms in backcountry settings: Studies of three rivers. *Journal of Leisure Research* 13(2):129-138.

Shelby, B. 1981b. Research, politics, and resource management decisions. *Leisure Sciences* 4(3).

Shelby, B. 1984. Estimating monetary values for use permits on western rivers. *Journal of Forestry* 82(2):107-109.

Shelby, B., and R.B. Colvin. 1979a. *Determining Use Levels for the Rogue River.* Water Resources Research Institute. WRRI-63. Corvallis: Oregon State University.

Shelby, B., and R.B. Colvin. 1979b. *Managing Use Levels on the Rogue River.* Corvallis: School of Forestry, Oregon State University.

Shelby, B., and R.B. Colvin. 1981a. *Carrying Capacity for the Illinois River.* Water Resources Research Institute. WRRI-72. Corvallis: Oregon State University.

Shelby, B., and R.B. Colvin. 1981b. Encounter measures in carrying capacity research: Actual, reported, and diary contacts. *Journal of Leisure Research* 14(4):350-360.

Shelby, B., and M.S. Danley. 1979. Scarcity, conflict, and equity in allocating public recreation resources. Paper presented at the annual meeting of the Rural Sociological Society. August. Burlington, Vermont.

Shelby, B., and M.S. Danley. 1980. *Allocating River Use.* USDA Forest Service Technical Report R-6-Rec-059.

Shelby, B., and R.L. Harris. 1985. Comparing methods for determining visitor evaluations of ecological impacts. *Journal of Leisure Research* 17(1)57-67.

Shelby, B., and R.L. Harris. 1986. User standards for ecological impacts at wilderness campsites. In *Proceedings of the National Wilderness Research Conference.*

Shelby, B., and T.A. Heberlein. 1984. A conceptual framework for carrying capacity determination. *Leisure Sciences* 6(4).

Shelby, B., T.A. Heberlein, J.J. Vaske, and G. Alfano. 1983. Expectations, preferences and feeling crowded in recreation activities. *Leisure Sciences.* 6(1):1-14.

Shelby, B., D. Lowney, and P. McKee. 1980. Problems with satisfaction as a criterion for management and change. Paper presented at the annual meeting of the Rural Sociological Society. Ithaca, New York.

Shelby, B., and J.M. Nielsen. 1976a. *Motors and Oars in Grand Canyon.* Colorado River Research Technical Report #3, Grand Canyon National Park, Arizona.

Shelby, B., and J.M. Nielsen. 1976b. *Private and Commercial Use in Grand Canyon.* Colorado River Research Technical Report #4. Grand Canyon National Park, Arizona.

Shelby, B., and J.M. Nielsen. 1976c. *Use Levels and Crowding in the Grand Canyon.* Colorado River Research Technical Report #2. Grand Canyon National Park, Arizona.

Shelby, B., and K. Stein. 1984. *Recreational Use and Carrying Capacity for the Klamath River.* Water Resources Research Institute. WRRI-92. Corvallis: Oregon State University.

Simon, H.A. 1956. Rational choice and the structure of the environment. *Psychological Review* 63:129.

Slovic, P., H. Kunreuther, and G.F. White. 1974. Decision process, rationality, and adjustment to natural hazards. In G.F. White (ed), *Natural Hazards: Local, Regional and Global*. New York: Oxford University Press.

Smith, V.K., and J.V. Krutilla. 1974. Simulation model for the management of low density recreational areas. *Journal of Environmental Economics and Management* 1:187-201.

Stankey, G.H. 1971. Myths in wilderness decision-making. *Journal of Soil and Water Conservation* 26(5):184-188.

Stankey, G.H. 1973. *Visitor Perception of Wilderness Recreation Carrying Capacity*. USDA Forest Service Research Paper INT-142. Ogden, Utah: Intermountain Forest and Range Experiment Station. 61 pp.

Stankey, G.H. 1974. Criteria for the determination of recreational carrying capacity in the Colorado River Basin. In A.B. Crawford and D.F. Peterson (eds.), *Environmental Management in the Colorado River Basin*. Logan: Utah State University Press.

Stankey, G.H. 1979. Use rationing in two southern California wildernesses. *Journal of Forestry* 77(5):347-349.

Stankey, G.H. 1980. Wilderness carrying capacity: Management and research progress in the United States. *Landscape Research* 5(3):6-11.

Stankey, G.H., and J. Baden. 1977. *Rationing Wilderness Use: Methods, Problems and Guidelines*. USDA Forest Service Research Paper INT-192. Ogden, Utah: Intermountain Forest and Range Experiment Station. 20 pp.

Stankey, G.H., and D.W. Lime. 1973. *Recreational Carrying Capacity: An Annotated Bibliography*. USDA Forest Service General Technical Report INT-3. Ogden, Utah: Intermountain Forest and Range Experiment Station. 45 pp.

Stankey, G.H., and S.F. McCool. 1984. Carrying capacity in recreational settings: Evolution, appraisal, and application. *Leisure Sciences* 6(4):453-474.

Stevens, J.S. 1978. Personal correspondence. Director, North Carolina State Parks.

Stockdale, J.E. 1978. Crowding: Determinants and effects. In L. Berkowitz (ed.), *Advances in Experimental Social Psychology*, Volume II. New York: Academic Press.

Stokols, D. 1972a. On the distinction between density and crowding: Some implications for future research. *Psychology Review* 79:275-277.

Stokols, D. 1972b. A social-psychological model of human crowding phenomena. Pages 105-132 in C.M. Loo (ed.), *Crowding and Behavior*. New York: MSS Information Corporation.

Stynes, D.J. 1977. Recreational carrying capacity and the management of dynamic systems. Paper presented at the National Recreation and Park Association Congress, October 2-6. Las Vegas, Nevada.

Tinsley, H.E.A., and R.A. Kass. 1978. Leisure activities and needs satisfaction: A replication and extension. *Journal of Leisure Research* 10(3):191-202.

Tivy, J. 1972. *The Concept and Determination of Carrying Capacity of Recreational Land in the USA*. Department of Geography, University of Glasgow, Scotland.

Vaske, J.J. 1977. The relationship of personal norms, social norms and reported contacts in Brule River visitors' perception of crowding. Masters thesis, University of Wisconsin, Madison.

Vaske, J.J. 1978. Contact-preference norms versus actual contacts: Crowding among Brule River canoers. Paper presented at the annual meeting of the Rural Sociological Society, August. San Francisco, California.

Vaske, J.J., and M.P. Donnelly. 1981. Two methodological approaches to recreational substitutability. Paper presented to the annual meeting of the Rural Sociological Society, August 23-25. Guelph, Ontario.

Vaske, J.J., and M.P. Donnelly. 1983. Hypothetical versus actual substitute choices. Paper presented at the Fifth Annual Southeastern Recreation Researcher Conference, February 18-19. Asheville, North Carolina.

Vaske, J.J., M.P. Donnelly, and T.A. Heberlein. 1980. Perceptions of crowding and resource quality by early and more recent visitors. *Leisure Sciences* 3(4):367-381.

Vaske, J.J., M.P. Donnelly, T.A. Heberlein, and B. Shelby. 1982. Differences in reported satisfaction ratings by consumptive and nonconsumptive recreationists. *Journal of Leisure Research* 14(3):195-206.

Vaske, J.J., A.R. Graefe, and F.R. Kuss. 1983. Recreation impacts: A synthesis of physical, environmental, and social research. Pages 96-107 in *Transactions* of the 48th North American Wildlife and Natural Resource Conference. Washington, D.C.: The Wildlife Management Institute.

Vaske, J.J., F.R. Kuss, and A.R. Graefe. 1984. *Recreation Impacts and Carrying Capacity: A Bibliography.* Department of Recreation, University of Maryland, College Park.

Verburg, K. 1977. *The Carrying Capacity of Recreational Lands: A Review.* Parks Canada. Planning, Prairie Regional Office. 57 pp.

Wagar, J.A. 1964. *The Carrying Capacity of Wildlands for Recreation.* Forest Service Monograph 2. Society of American Foresters. 23 pp.

Wagar, J.A. 1966. Quality in outdoor recreation. *Trends in Parks and Recreation* 3(3):9-12.

Wagar, J.A. 1974. Recreational carrying capacity reconsidered. *Journal of Forestry* 72(3):274-278.

Wagar, J.V.K. 1946. Services and facilities for forest recreationists. *Journal of Forestry* 44(11).

Walster, E., E. Berscheid, and G.W. Walster. 1973. New directions in equity research. *Journal of Personality and Social Psychology* 25(2).

Washburn, R.F. 1982. Wilderness recreational carrying capacity: Are numbers necessary? *Journal of Forestry* 80(1):726-728.

Weiss, C.H. (editor). 1977. *Using Social Research in Public Policy-Making.* Lexington, Massachusetts: Lexington Books.

Weiss, C.H., and M.J. Bucuvalas. 1980. Truth tests and utility tests: Decision makers frames of reference for social science research. *American Sociological Review* 45 (April):302-313.

Wildavsky, A. 1964. *The Politics of the Budgetary Process*. Boston: Little, Brown and Co.

Wildavsky, A. 1979. *Speaking Truth to Power*. Boston: Little, Brown and Co.

Winsborough, H.H. 1965. The social consequences of high population density. *Law and Contemporary Problems* 30(1):120-126.

Whitam, M. 1978. Personal communication. Assistant Director, Oregon Department of Parks and Recreation.

Wolfle, D. 1970. Chance or human judgment? *Science* 167(3922).

Index

Social capacity studies: determining need for, 144-145; and experience definition, 145

Social efficiency, 114-115

Social norms: in recreation, 17; and contact preference standards, 75

Use conflict, 22

Use levels: and the descriptive component, 12; and impacts, 14; relation to management parameters, 21; and impact parameters, 23; and encounters, 30; at study sites, 31; mea-surement of, 31, 126-127; and contacts, 38-39; and satisfaction, 52; and perceived crowding, 68; variations in, 127-128; and carrying capacity studies, 139-140

User preferences, 17-18

Value judgments: and optimum carrying capacity, 9; and value conflicts, 9

Visitor impact management, 97

Willingness to pay, 47-49